THE CAPITOLINE MUSEUMS
GUIDE

ROMA CAPITALE

ASSESSORATO
ALLA CULTURA E AL TURISMO

SOVRINTENDENZA CAPITOLINA
AI BENI CULTURALI

Electa

Cover
Opus sectile panel
from the Basilica of Giunio Basso,
detail
(Photographic Archive
of the Capitoline Museums,
photograph by Araldo De Luca)

ROMA

Assessorato Cultura e Turismo
Sovrintendenza Capitolina ai Beni Culturali

Ignazio Roberto Marino
Mayor

Giovanna Marinelli
Councillor for Culture and Tourism

Sovrintendenza ai Beni Culturali

Claudio Parisi Presicce
Capitoline Superintendent
for Cultural Heritage

Claudio Parisi Presicce, Director
Museums Direction
and Operative Unit for
the Archaeological Museums
Polo Grande Campidoglio

Texts
Margherita Albertoni, Paolo Arata,
Maddalena Cima, Maria Dell'Era,
Elena Bianca Di Gioia,
Laura Ferrea, Sergio Guarino,
Antonella Magagnini,
Patrizia Masini, Marina Mattei,
Maria Cristina Molinari,
Anna Mura Sommella,
Claudio Parisi Presicce, Micaela
Perrone, Emilia Talamo,
Daniela Velestino

Photographs
Photographic Archive
of the Capitoline Museums
(photographs by Alessandra
Ciniglio,
Zeno Colantoni, Araldo
De Luca, Lorenzo De Masi,
Antonio Idini, Roberto Lucignani,
Barbara Malter, Attilio Maranzano,
Pietro Mari, Maria Teresa Natale,
Maurizio Necci, Pasquale Rizzi,
Alessandro Vasari)
Maurizio Di Ianni
Chromamedia for Zètema
(Ph. A. Panegrossi and P. Cipollina)

Illustrations and surveys
Studio Inklink, Patricia S. Lulof,
Studio R.A.M. snc

The guide was edited
for Electa
by Nunzio Giustozzi

Graphic design
smART
Sebastiano Girardi
with Miriam Nonino

Editing and layout
in.pagina srl, Mestre-Venice

Translation by
Darius A. Arya, Tina Cawthra,
Silvia Mari and Salvatore Mele

The architectural project
of the new spaces is
by the architect
Carlo Aymonino
The preparation project
is by the architect
Francesco Stefanori

Zètema
progetto cultura

Albino Ruberti
President and Chief Executive
Officer

Roberta Biglino
General Manager

Laura Silvestro
Editorial service, bookshop and
merchandising

Reprint 2015
New expanded edition 2006

© Roma Capitale
Assessorato alla Cultura
e al Turismo
Sovrintendenza Capitolina
ai Beni Culturali
Zètema Progetto Cultura s.r.l.

Editorial project of
Mondadori Electa S.p.A., Milan

www.electaweb.com

Equestrian statue of the Emperor
Marcus Aurelius, detail

The Capitoline Hill

Walking up the monumental ramp (*cordonata*), one comes upon the piazza of the
Capitoline Hill (*Campidoglio*), a remarkable architectural project designed by
Michelangelo. This space also represents the outcome of a history spanning 1000 years,
which singled out the Capitoline Hill as the religious and political center of the city.
In the beginning a small, central valley characterized the hill and divided two wooded rises,
the *Arx* and *Capitolium*. Legendary tradition locates in this valley the mythic *Asylum*,
instituted by Romulus for gathering the inhabitants from nearby populations. Today, in
light of archaeological research conducted (and still in progress) in the area comprised by
the Palazzo dei Conservatori (Palace of the Conservators), the legendary stories handed
down concerning the origins of the city appear scientifically more documentable and closer
to historical reality than ever. In fact, the archaeological strata regarding the most ancient
phase of the Capitoline Hill show traces of inhabitation on the hill, beginning at the end
of the Bronze Age (1200-1000 BC). These important archaeological studies (still in the
preliminary stages) recognize faint traces of a settlement. Some burials of children and
the remains of the widespread production of metal-based handcrafts belong to the site.
In the historical period, the Capitoline Hill appeared as the one and only sacred acropolis
of the city. The last kings of the Roman tradition, the Tarquins, built the Temple of
Capitoline Jupiter on the *Capitolium*. However, the temple was not dedicated until the first
year of the Republican era, 509 BC. The temple became the symbol of Roman civilization,
replicated in all of the new cities founded by Rome. It was the destination of the triumphal
ceremonies held in honor of victorious generals upon their return to Rome. The long
triumphal procession winded through the city, exhibiting prisoners and spoils of war along
the Via Sacra and up to the Temple of Jupiter, in whose name campaigns of conquest were
undertaken. Recent archaeological surveys have revealed the imposing foundations of the
temple, perfectly preserved and incorporated into the structures of the sixteenth century
Palazzo Caffarelli. The Temple of Juno Moneta, site of the mint of the Roman State, stood
on the *Arx*, the rise that tradition assigned to the Sabine population and on which today
stands the impressive structure of the Basilica of the Aracoeli.
At the end of the Republican period, the construction of massive structures of the
Tabularium, which housed the Archives of the Roman State, regularized the slopes of the
Capitoline Hill facing the Forum. The imposing building did not alter the preexisting
Temple of Jupiter Veiovis (196 BC), characterized by a transverse axis. The mysterious
divinity related to Jupiter and the underworld was the recipient of the cult. Many other
temples on the Capitoline affirmed the sacredness of the hill.
In the Republican period the construction of public buildings shows the competition for
supremacy that existed among the most important noble Roman families. Beyond the
Temple of Capitoline Jupiter, the ancient sources attest to the existence of other sanctuaries
in the area dedicated to *Jupiter Feretrius, Fides, Mens, Venus Erycina, Ops, Jupiter Tonans,
Mars Ultor,* and *Jupiter Custos*. In the mediaeval period, the ancient buildings fell into
disuse, but the memory of the ancient greatness was recorded in the description of the

Jacques Carlu,
view of the *Capitolium* dominated
by the Temple of Capitoline Jupiter
(1924)

Mirabilia: "*Capitolium* is thus named because it was the head of the entire world and because Consuls and Senators lived there in order to govern the city and the world. High, solid walls entirely encrusted with glass and gold and marvelously engraved works protected its face. At the center of the citadel rose a palace, entirely decorated with gold and precious stones, that seems to have been worth one third of the entire world [...]."
The Corsi family transformed the structures of the *Tabularium* into a stronghold. First Henry IV (1084) then Pasquale II (1105) chased away the Corsi family in order to prevent a dangerous, alternative center of power from forming there. In 1130, through the decree of Anacletus II, the Benedictines of the Aracoeli became the proprietors of the Capitoline Hill. During the entire mediaeval period, the architectural history of the Capitoline Hill overlapped with the vicissitudes of the municipal institutions. In 1143-1144 – the year of the birth of the Municipality of Rome – an antipapal revolution (*renovatio Senatus*) installed on the Capitoline Hill a collegial magistracy composed of fifty Senators invested with public and judicial functions. At the beginning of the thirteenth century the magistracy that was composed of one or two Senators, assisted by a Municipal Board with deliberative power, substituted the collegial magistracy. In 1299, the opening of a loggia (covered terrace) facing the piazza that hosted the market transformed the Palazzo Senatorio. This action thus confirmed the overturning of the topographical situation: whereas in the Roman period, the principal monuments on the hill faced the monumental center of the city (i.e., towards the Forum), in the mediaeval period the Capitoline Hill faced the Campus Martius. In 1363, the first public statutes defined the form of government chosen by the city, i.e., a single foreign Senator assisted by three elected magistrates, the Conservators, representatives of the new social classes in power.
In the fifteenth century, the Palazzo Senatorio appeared as a fortress with towers, constructed by Boniface IX (1389-1404), Martin V (1427), and Nicholas V (1447-1455). The palace façade, with a double staircase, facing the piazza had three Guelph-cross windows and a loggia on the second floor. This period also witnessed the transformation of the Palace of the Banderesi (i.e., Captains of the public *militia*) into the monumental premises of the

Anonymous drawing
from the middle of the sixteenth
century, the Capitoline "plain"

Conservators. Documents of the fifteenth century attribute this construction to Nicholas V. Cohabitation between the municipal institutions and the papacy was not always peaceful. In the meanwhile, the distinction between the Capitoline Hill as a place of memory and Vatican as a place of the pontifical power became clear. In 1471, Sixtus IV ennobled the function of the Capitoline Hill through a donation to the People of Rome. He gave large bronze statues that had been housed in the patriarch's Lateran residence. This act brought about the creation of the oldest public museum in the world. The She-wolf, placed on the façade of the Palazzo dei Conservatori, became the symbol of the city. The colossal bronze portrait of Constantine with the *"palla Sansonis"* was placed in the external portico. Architecturally, the Capitoline "plain" remained virtually unchanged until 1537. In this year, Paul III Farnese commissioned Michelangelo to transfer the equestrian statue of Marcus Aurelius from the Lateran to the Capitoline and to systematize it in the center of the piazza. The statue had escaped the normal fate of ancient bronze statues because in the mediaeval period it was believed that it represented Constantine, the first Christian emperor. The papal project, fiercely opposed by the Lateran canons and, it seems, Michelangelo himself, was completed in the following year. The presence and the strong visual effect of the statue, extraordinarily charged with symbolic significance and historical importance, created a new fulcrum at the center of the piazza and forever changed the aspect of the piazza on the Capitoline Hill. The pope entrusted the systematization of the area to the ingenious Michelangelo. Plans, probably under way during the period of the transfer of the colossal bronze statue of Marcus Aurelius, took shape in the following decades. The project was not

Jeronymus Cock,
the piazza on the Capitoline Hill
(1562)

finished until more than a century later, with the completion of the Palazzo Nuovo (New Palace). Renovation began with the Palazzo Senatorio. The palace preserves, within its structure, the ancient remains of the *Tabularium*, and mediaeval and Renaissance period structures, all of which symbolize its uninterrupted building phases. An imposing façade transformed the palace on the side facing the square. Large-scale pilasters and a double monumental staircase divided the façade. The staircase gave access to the "noble floor," which earlier had housed a loggia and the hall of the Senator. Then, the installation of a fountain enriched the façade. In addition, colossal statues representing Rivers, found at the beginning of the century on the Quirinal, flanked the fountain. Since 1513 the statues, depicted in a lying pose, had been arranged on the square to face the façade of the Palazzo dei Conservatori. Finally, in a niche at the center of the façade, came the addition of an ancient porphyry statue of seated Minerva, transformed into the goddess Roma through the addition of attributes typical of the deity. Thus, the decorative program was complete in 1588.

The transformation of the Palazzo dei Conservatori began in 1563, under the pontificate of Pius IV. A long portico with colonnaded arcades characterized the original façade. The presence of two of the most prestigious works from the Capitoline collections, the She-wolf and the colossal bronze head of Constantine, distinguished the façade. The She-wolf replaced the lion as the civic symbol of the city. In the mediaeval period first it was located in front of the Palazzo Senatorio and then was moved inside "in a covered loggia

Palazzo dei Conservatori,
Hall of the Geese: representation
of games conducted
on the piazza of the Capitoline Hill

overlooking the city plain" (Aldrovandi). The addition of a pair of twins transformed the
statue from a symbol of justice, while in the Lateran, to *Mater Romanorum*. The colossal
head was relocated to the courtyard, where the number of monuments increased year after
year to enrich the Capitoline collections of antiquity. The project by Michelangelo was
completed only after his death. This project strengthened the fifteenth century structure
of the palace through a geometrical design, which was articulated by a large-scale order
of Corinthian pilasters. The plan also regularized the form of the courtyard and inserted,
within the building, a large, monumental staircase, to reach the upper story. This staircase
replaced an external staircase in the courtyard, visible in some ancient drawings. In
addition, in some parts, it modified the internal layout of the rooms. A well-balanced,
extraordinary urban plan took into account the slightly deviating course of the structure of
the palace in relation to the façade of the Palazzo Senatorio and in respect to the central
axis of the piazza, marked by the equestrian statue of Marcus Aurelius. This divergent
course suggested that the architectural design of the piazza needed to be completed by
the construction of a twin palace on the opposite side. This new palace had to be equally
divergent in such a way as to accompany the gaze of one who ascended the redesigned
monumental ramp (*cordonata*) originating from the Campus Martius towards the Palazzo
Senatorio. A series of engravings (dating to 1567-1569) by Etienne Dupérac attest to the
conception of the project, which found its logical conclusion only through the construction
of the Palazzo Nuovo. Until that time a large retaining wall for the enormous Basilica of the
Aracoeli delimited the left side of the piazza.
In 1596, according to the drawing of Giacomo della Porta, the installation of the impressive

Colossal statue
of one of the Dioscouri
on the balustrade
of the piazza on the Capitoline Hill

The piazza on the Capitoline Hill
now

fountain of the Marforio decorated this side of the piazza. However, construction of the structure began only in 1603, under the pontificate of Clement VIII. With little variation the building adhered to the original design conceived by Michelangelo. In 1667, after difficult building episodes, Pope Alexander VII oversaw the completion of the building. However, the new museum, destined to house the Capitoline collections of antiquity, was not dedicated until 1734 (the pontificate of Clement XII). In this period, the piazza of the Capitoline Hill reached its definitive configuration. Two colossal statues of the Dioscouri, found in the vicinity of the Ghetto, the imposing "Trophies of Marius," removed from the large, monumental fountain on the Esquiline, and the statues of Constantine and his son Constantine II, transferred from the Aracoeli, enriched the balustrade that faced the Campus Martius. The precious star-shaped pavement design was the last element required for the completion of the project designed by Michelangelo. Although not constructed until 1940, it appears in Dupérac's engravings. The isolation of the entire Capitoline Hill and the large-scale intervention that created a large subterranean gallery to join the three palaces facing the piazza provided an opportunity to install the pavement inspired by, although not perfectly adherent to, Michelangelo's design. Construction of the pavement closed the chapter on the creation of a single architectural space that was fully coherent and "perfect," after centuries of elaboration and adjustments. It is for this reason that the Capitoline Hill represents a museum complex of extraordinary historical and cultural significance. The piazza, the palaces, the archaeological and historical-artistic collections, and now, with the reopening of the subterranean gallery, also the principal ancient monuments constitute organic and harmonious elements of the museum complex.

Palazzo dei Conservatori,
Hall of the Eagles:
the piazza on the Capitoline Hill

The Formation of the Collections

Beginning in the fifteenth century, the formation of the Capitoline Museums of antiquity
was characterized by new interest in the archaeological patrimony of ancient Rome as
the object of antiquarianism and collecting, rather than the object of potential reuse.
In 1471, Pope Sixtus IV donated four very famous bronze sculptures – the She-wolf, the
Spinario (boy pulling a thorn out of his foot), the Camillus, and the bronze head of
Constantine with hand and globe – until that moment exhibited in front of the
patriarch's Lateran residence. Because of their location in the Lateran, they symbolized
the continuity between Imperial Rome and the temporal power of the Church. The
donation marks the beginning of the return of ancient sculptural works to the Capitoline
Hill and the birth of the Capitoline Museum complex. In fact, centuries of devastation
and abandonment, followed by the collapse of the Roman Empire, had despoiled the hill
of temples, honorary arches, and statues that had rendered famous the *Capitolium
fulgens*, recorded with amazement by Roman authors of the late-antique period. The
works constituted the *thesaurus Romanitatis*, a sort of inheritance from the ancient world
that the Church had collected and jealously guarded during the entire mediaeval period.
Through this strongly symbolic gesture, the works returned to the People of Rome to be
located on the hill representative of Rome's sacred past.
A long inscription, still preserved to this day and located at the entrance of the Palazzo
dei Conservatori, records the details of this event. The inscription documents the
important moment of the creation of the Capitoline Museum complex, by citing the

Marten van Heemskerck,
detail of the view
of the Capitoline Hill
with the statue of a River god
in front of the portico
of the Palazzo dei Conservatori

generous donation that, "*ob immensam benignitatem,*" Sixtus IV gave to the People of Rome. The text indicates wisely that this was not a simple donation but, rather, a true "restitution" of the remarkable works of bronze, testimony of the ancient magnificence of the People of Rome who had created them: "*Aeneas insignes statuas – priscae excellentiae virtutisque monumentum – Romano populo unde exorte fuere restituendas condonandasque censuit.*"

Sixtus IV's precious gift was clearly intended to confirm the predominance of the pontifical power on the Capitoline Hill, through the consecration of this ancient hill as an important symbol of ancient Rome. This act contrasted with the role attributed to the Capitoline Hill as the central proponent of civic independence, tenaciously defended by the magistracy of the Capitoline. In this way, a confrontation began (utilizing symbolic language) between the papal power and the Municipality of Rome. This confrontation brought about, in the span of a century, the total transformation of the piazza of the Capitoline Hill. Two sixteenth century views, one, a drawing by Marten van Heemskerck, and the other, a fresco in the Hall of the Eagles in the Palazzo dei Conservatori, document with great accuracy the condition of the Capitoline area during the first half of the sixteenth century. At this time, the mediaeval configuration still characterized the area. In addition, the small fresco attests to the beginning of the process of transformation, determined by the transfer of the equestrian statue of Marcus Aurelius from the Lateran in 1538. The statue became the focal point of the architectural systematization of the piazza, according to the will of Paul III and designed by Michelangelo.

The piazza on the Capitoline Hill with the Palazzo dei Conservatori in a fresco in the Hall of the Triumphs

The statuary group of "A lion attacking a horse" appears in the drawing of Heemskerck, only a few years older than the fresco, in its mediaeval location, at the top of the stairs of access to the Palazzo Senatorio. This work, the symbol of juridical power of senatorial authority, was the only ancient sculpture present on the Capitoline Hill before the Sixtus IV's donation. The statue characterized the *locus iustitiae*, already recorded in fourteenth century documents, where it was common to pronounce and, sometimes carry out, capital sentences. With the systematization of the façade of the Palazzo Senatorio, on the occasion of the monumental transformation of the piazza on the Capitoline Hill, this statue group became part of the Capitoline collections of antiquity.

In the same drawing, in addition to the bronze head of Constantine located within the arcades, the statue of the She-wolf appears on the façade of the Palazzo dei Conservatori, transferred according to the will of Sixtus IV from the *campus Lateranensis*. Before 1509, an anonymous artist added the figures of the twins. This intervention definitively cancelled the ominous characteristic of the symbol of justice that the She-wolf had had in the Lateran, and, instead, underlined the symbol of *Mater Romanorum*, more appropriate for a work that already had become the emblem of the municipality's power. In the period between the date of the drawing (1532-1537) and that of the fresco (1541-1543), the She-wolf was transferred inside the palace "*in porticu interiori prope aulam*," i.e., in the portico located on the far right of the palace, next to the main room now called the Hall "of the Horatii and Curiatii."

Important works of ancient sculpture reached the Capitoline Hill between the end of the fifteenth century and the first half of the sixteenth century, creating a remarkable collection in front of the Palazzo dei Conservatori. This antiquarian patrimony of enormous historical and artistic value confirmed the role of the Capitoline as a public museum of antiquity. The Conservators purchased the bronze statue of Hercules found in the Forum Boarium during the papacy of Sixtus IV. The statue played a very important role among the first works of art destined to augment the original nucleus of bronze statues donated by Sixtus IV. The Conservators displayed the statue on a high

Stefano della Bella,
the courtyard
of the Palazzo
dei Conservatori

base in front of their palace, as a "monument of the glory of Rome." This statue is a copy
of a Greek original dating to the fourth century BC. It was successively moved first to the
courtyard, where Heemskerck saw it, and then transferred inside the palace, into the
Conservators' Apartment (cf. U. Aldrovandi, *Delle statue antiche che per tutta Roma in
diversi luoghi e case si veggono*, Venice 1556, p. 273).
In 1513, two colossal statues of river divinities, found in the Baths of Constantine on
the Quirinal, were placed on either side of the palace entrance. In 1588-1589, these
sculptures, dating to the Trajanic period, constituted part of the sculptural group located
on the monumental staircase that acts as an entrance to the Palazzo Senatorio.
A little while later (1515) came the acquisition of the three large, high relief panels
decorated with scenes related to the life of Marcus Aurelius. They originally pertained
to the sculptural decoration that adorned a monument celebrating the emperor on the
occasion of his triumph in 176 AD. These reliefs signify one of the highest expressions of
sculpture of historical character that Roman art has passed down to us. They represent
the submission of the barbarians, the triumph, and sacrifice before the Temple of
Capitoline Jupiter. In addition, the reliefs are documents of exceptional value destined
to represent the ideal continuity between the ancient world and the Renaissance-period
Capitoline Hill. At the beginning of the sixteenth century, thanks to the works of F.
Albertini, *Opusculum de Mirabilibus*, in 1510, and Fulvio, *Antiquaria Urbis*, in 1513,
we know with sufficient precision the display of the Capitoline collections.

In fact, we know that at the beginning of the sixteenth century a great part of the sculptures were arranged within the Palazzo dei Conservatori, whereas the large-scale statues were located in the courtyard of the same building. The courtyard, which today we see in its eighteenth century phase, has been modified in respect to the Renaissance phase through the addition of a portico along the wall facing the entrance. The "Cesi Roma" and the statues of the barbarians in *bigio* marble were located in the portico. On the right side of the courtyard, stood the Hercules from the Forum Boarium and the remains of the great acrolith of Constantine from the Basilica of Maxentius. On the left side, stood the three reliefs of Marcus Aurelius, which Leo X transferred from the Church of Santi Luca e Martina in the Roman Forum. In 1594, the head of the acrolith of Constantine was transferred to the pediment located over the fountain of Marforio, as decoration of the retaining wall of the Church of the Aracoeli. A drawing by Stefano della Bella attests that the colossal head returned definitively to the courtyard of the Palazzo dei Conservatori in 1659.

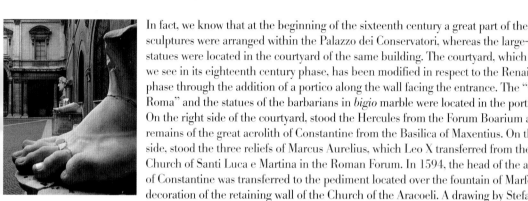

Fragments of Constantine's colossal statue in the courtyard of the Palazzo dei Conservatori before the restoration

In 1541, a colossal statue of Athena, found and donated to the city magistracy during the papacy of Paul III, occupied a niche in front of the entrance, on the central axis of the courtyard. Shortly thereafter (under the papacy of Sixtus V), the statue became the center of a lively *querelle* (controversy) when it was used as a central element in the decoration of the large staircase designed by Michelangelo for the Palazzo Senatorio. The over life-sized sculpture had already been removed from the back wall of the courtyard to permit the installation of the *Fasti Consolari* fragments. The fragments came to light in the Roman Forum in 1546. A few years later, Cardinal Farnese donated them to the People of Rome. Onofrio Panvinio records that Michelangelo himself assisted in the recomposition and architectural arrangement of the recovered fragments at the Capitoline. The *Fasti* of the Capitoline, transferred in 1583 to the Hall of the She-wolf (where they remain today), were reassembled according to Michelangelo's design. However, during this systematization, major readjustments modified his overall plan.

Available documentation regarding the oldest account of the collection describes the situation of the Capitoline collections on the eve of two extraordinary events, which determined a radical transformation of the collections. First, in 1563, work began on the restructuring of the Palazzo dei Conservatori and the subsequent resystematization of the works of art housed within the palace. Second, in 1566, Pius V donated works of art to the People of Rome with the intention of "purging the Vatican of pagan idols." Initially, the pope had intended to donate 150 statues from the Vatican collections, but he substantially revised his plan. Nevertheless, a considerable number of works, originally housed in the Theater of the Belvedere, reached the Capitoline Hill and enriched the "statuary collection," subsequently housed on the ground floor of the Palazzo dei Conservatori. In addition, according to the engravings of Dupérac, some statues were displayed on the old bell tower and on the façade of the Palazzo Senatorio, in accordance with Michelangelo's design.

Restructuring of the Palazzo dei Conservatori finally permitted a suitable arrangement of the works already in the Capitoline collection and other works subsequently donated or

Palazzo dei Conservatori,
Hall of the She-wolf

purchased. Sculptures of great prestige became part of the collections in the second half of the sixteenth century. Among these are the two statues of Julius Caesar and Navarca, the Capitoline Brutus, and the *Lex de imperio Vespasiani*. In 1568 the Hall of the Horatii and Curiatii housed this extraordinary relic and the hand and globe of Constantine (originally located in the external portico of the palace). The entirely restructured courtyard housed the large sarcophagus of Alexander Severus, acquired in 1590, and the statue group of "A lion attacking a horse" (restored on this occasion by Ruggero Bescapè).

After the completion of the renovations in the Palazzo dei Conservatori, the Marcus Aurelius reliefs went to a new location; they became immured on the second floor landing of the staircase, where they are located to this day.

Many years later, the two colossal statues of the Dioscouri, found in 1560, were placed on the balustrade that encloses the piazza. The erection of the statues on their respective pedestals was very difficult because of their fragmentary state. Indeed, a demanding restoration of the statues, initiated in 1582, lasted several years. In 1590, under the papacy of Sixtus V, the so-called "Trophies of Marius" were transferred to the Capitoline to embellish the balustrade that encloses the piazza on the end facing the large ramp (*cordonata*). In antiquity the "Trophies" had decorated the monumental fountain created by Alexander Severus on the Esquiline. In 1590, two Egyptian lions were also placed on the foot of the ramp.

Palazzo Nuovo,
Hall of the Emperors

Michaelis reports that, "the seventeenth century was as unproductive, regarding the augmentation of the collection, as the sixteenth century was productive." In fact, diffuse private collections and the birth of the great collections of patrician palaces absorbed the best finds available on the antiquarian market. A drawing by Stefano della Bella, completed after 1659, gives an idea of the overcrowding that characterized the courtyard. Likewise, the Palazzo dei Conservatori was so full of statues that it was very difficult for the ancient civic magistracy, which utilized these spaces as an official and representative seat, to execute its functions.

In 1603 construction of the Palazzo Nuovo on the left side of the square began under Pope Clement VIII. Fifty years later, Carlo Rainaldi finally completed the palace.

The Palazzo Nuovo became a museum only in 1733, when Clement XII purchased the Albani Collection. In the preceding decades, this building already hosted conspicuous numbers of statues that had originated in the Palazzo dei Conservatori. The Palazzo Nuovo housed this collection and the principal nucleus of the Albani Collection, which was characterized by an exceptional compilation of portraits of famous men, philosophers, and emperors. In 1734, immediately after the dedication of the museum, Clement XII and Benedict XIV gave further donations.

Numerous works of art, including the Capitoline Gaul (1734), the Satyr in *rosso antico* marble (1746), the group of Amor and Psyche and, finally, the famous Capitoline Venus

(1750) already in private collections or recently discovered, eventually enriched the rooms decorated with the crests of Innocent X and Alexander VII.

In 1744, Benedict XIV donated the marble *Forma Urbis*, created in the Severan period. It was arranged in 26 panels along the large staircase that ascended to the first floor of the museum. This exceptional historical-topographical document, discovered two centuries before near the Church of Santi Cosma e Damiano, remained in the Capitoline Museum until the beginning of the twentieth century. The two Centaurs in *bigio morato*, arranged at the center of the Great Hall, and the very refined Mosaic of the Doves, number among the most recent precious acquisitions of the museum. All of them were found in the villa of the Emperor Hadrian in Tivoli. Clement XIII donated them in the second half of the eighteenth century.

The Capitoline Museum represents a remarkable testimony of eighteenth century museum display whose original context has remained intact. The almost unaltered state of the eighteenth century museum is perceptible through a comparison between the rooms and the drawings of the rooms executed in the eighteenth and nineteenth centuries. The engraving of Natoire (1759), depicting the lobby of the museum and the courtyard, records the fountain of the Marforio in its new eighteenth century location. The lithograph of Benoist (1870) depicts the gilded bronze statue of Hercules, previously located in the courtyard of the Palazzo dei Conservatori, in the area facing the Gallery. The original arrangement of the works of art into categories and particular criteria necessitated by restoration determined the layout of the works within the rooms. In addition, the reconstruction and the interpretation of the ancient sculptures highlight the particular character of the collection as a testimony of the learned collecting that took place over the past centuries.

In 1771, the dedication of the Pius-Clement Museum in the Vatican marked a static moment in the efforts to augment the archaeological collections in the Capitoline. In fact, the popes paid singular attention, from that moment on, to the new museum. The situation became dramatic for the museum complex of the Capitoline when, as a result of the Treaty of Tolentino in 1797, many of the most famous works from the civic collections were transferred to France. After the fall of Napoleon, in 1815, only the tenacious intervention of Canova brought back the principal works of art to Italy. In this way, the *Spinario*, Brutus, Capitoline Venus, and the Dying Gaul were able to return to their original locations.

In 1838, according to the will of Gregory XVI, the civic magistracy regained the Capitoline Museum. However, simultaneously it was deprived of the rich collection of Egyptian sculptures. In exchange, it gained some works, including the Amendola sarcophagus and the Velletri-type Athena. The acquisitions made in the first seventy years of the nineteenth century were few but significant. Particularly relevant is the group of large bronzes found in Vicolo delle Palme in Trastevere (1848), the collection of Greek and Etruscan vases donated by Augusto Castellani and especially the collection of ancient coins that eventually constituted the principal nucleus of the Capitoline Medal Collection. The year 1870 marked the transfer of the capital of the new Reign of Italy to

Palazzo Nuovo,
Great Hall

Rome, and the vicissitudes at the end of the nineteenth century marked a fundamental milestone in the life and development of the city.

The transformation and enlargement of the Capitoline Museum complex reflected the events in a very obvious manner. In fact, even the arrangement of the archaeological collections, located in the Palazzo Nuovo (the repository of a large collection of ancient sculpture), underwent a profound change. Indeed, the formulation of scientific criteria (made possible by the relevant contribution of material found during the excavations in the urban environment) substituted the prevalent antiquarian character of the collections formed through donations and acquisitions. The new political class generated feverish building activity and related excavation works in vast areas of the periphery in order to bestow the capital with public buildings and residential quarters due to new exigencies. In fact, this agenda brought to light an enormous amount of archaeological material. In this way, a new section of the museum in the Palazzo dei Conservatori developed. The palace lost its function as the official seat of the homonymous civic magistracy. In addition, it had enough room to house a wooden pavilion for a temporary presentation of the works of art found during the great excavations conducted in the urban surroundings.

In 1903, Rodolfo Lanciani oversaw the enlargement and new systematization of this sector of the museum of the Palazzo dei Conservatori. He made it possible to obtain a better organization of the material according to new museological criteria, aimed at underlying the importance of the data obtained from excavations. Therefore, the works were distributed in the rooms according to their provenience, privileging a more articulated interpretation of the archaeological data rather than an "antiquarian" vision that tended to underline the aesthetic value of the sculptures as masterpieces of the ancient art.

The years of the Governorship, in particular between 1925 and 1930, witnessed a profound renewal of the Capitoline Museum structures. The change ushered in the creation of a new museum section through the acquisition of the Palazzo Caffarelli, previously owned by the Austrians. Sculptural works of art, found in the nineteenth century and transferred on this occasion from the Municipal Antiquarium on the Caelian Hill, enriched the new museum section. At first, this structure was named the Mussolini Museum and later assumed the title, the Museo Nuovo. In this case, the arrangement of the works did not follow the new topographic systematization that Lanciani desired for the Museum of the Palazzo dei Conservatori. Instead, it followed a display criterion intended to reproduce the most significant milestones of Greek art through Roman copies inspired by Greek originals. At the same time, in 1929, the exhibition spaces in the new Antiquarium on the Caelian Hill were enlarged and completely renovated. The displays centered on the testimonies relative to the most ancient history of the city, from the origins to the Republican age. The Antiquarium also features objects of daily life in Rome dating to the Imperial period.

After this period of renewal of the Capitoline Museum structures, welcomed by the contemporary academic world with great enthusiasm, new serious problems arose concerning the collections placed under the jurisdiction of the Governorship. Two factors addressed the urgency of finding new spaces for the enlargement of the museum site. First, the premises of the Antiquarium on the Caelian Hill after 1939 were unfit for use. Second, a noteworthy quantity of materials of great artistic and scientific relevance was found in various parts of the city (in particular, around the slopes of the Capitoline during the isolation of the hill).

Only in 1956, the creation of a new section of the Palazzo dei Conservatori, the Braccio Nuovo (New Wing) permitted the exposition of very important sculptures. The sculptures belonged to Republican and early Imperial monuments found on the slopes of the Capitoline Hill and during the excavations conducted in Largo Argentina. During the same period, the underground gallery located beneath the piazza of the Capitoline Hill was utilized as an exposition space for the Epigraphic Collection. The gallery constitutes an extraordinary axis linking the Palazzo dei Conservatori, the Palazzo Nuovo, and the Palazzo Senatorio (that contains the *Tabularium* and the Temple of Veiovis). The history of the Capitoline collections, which seems to have obtained its definitive form through post-war regulations, continued to develop. Indeed, the continuation of studies and research conducted within the museum and its numerous storerooms in these last decades led to important acquisitions of works of art and sculptural groups and the need for new presentations of previously studied material.

The restructuring of the Capitoline Museums that took place in distinct periods over a long span of time resulted in the recovery and creation of new spaces within the museum

The piazza of the Capitoline Hill
from the tower
of the Palazzo Senatorio

complex itself and the creation of a new decentralized museum site, the Montemartini Power Plant. During the restructuring of the Museo Nuovo, the discovery of the massive remains of the Temple of Capitoline Jupiter within the rooms rendered impossible the reorganization of these museum spaces according to the old arrangement. The Montemartini Power Plant, initially destined to provide a temporary display space for the Capitoline collections, instead, became the permanent site of a section of the collections because it is an ideal place to present sculptures to the public. The exceptionally large dimensions and luminosity of the spaces, and the striking contrast between the perfectly preserved machinery of the old electric power station and the brightness of the classical sculptures, constitute irremissible ingredients for the full utilization of an extraordinary artistic patrimony. The architectural complex of the Temple of Apollo Sosianus, recently reassembled in its former monumental composition (due to the availability of suitable spaces), has a very important place in this patrimony.

Now that the exhibition space at the Capitoline Museums has been enlarged and the collections have been reorganized within the Palazzo dei Conservatori and the Clementino Caffarelli complex, the Marcus Aurelius equestrian group has been included in the museum, the sculptural complexes are presented coherently and have been reorganized following accurate historical and archival research, and a novel exhibition of material relating to the ancient Capitoline Hill has been put together.

Hall of the Faun

Palazzo Nuovo

The palace located on the left of the piazza originally bore the name "Nuovo" (New) because it was constructed after the Palazzo Senatorio and the Palazzo dei Conservatori. Sixteenth century artwork depicts in its place a retaining wall of the Convent of the Aracoeli that, today, overlooks the crowning of the internal courtyard. From the beginning, Michelangelo Buonarroti included the Palazzo Nuovo in the general design of his project. However, the palace was built after his death, and it was completed in several phases in the span of almost two centuries. The first stone was laid in 1603, under the auspices of Clement VIII. He entrusted the work to Girolamo Rainaldi, architect of the People of Rome. In 1614, only the foundations were complete. After a long pause, work began anew only in 1654, under the pontificate of Innocent X, who commissioned Carlo Rainaldi. He did his utmost to complete the construction of the building. From the beginning, the Palazzo Nuovo was destined to host famous masterpieces of Greek and Roman sculpture (already present in conspicuous numbers on the hill) in niches and aedicules, according to criteria "of the ancients." Drawings and written documents attest to the importance of the Palazzo Nuovo. In fact, the building was the first to house an antiquarian patrimony of public property. For this reason, the palace was conceived as a division of external and internal spaces to optimally emphasize marbles located along the walls in gabled niches and intentionally open aedicules. The new building differs architecturally from the palaces of the Roman aristocracy that, already by the end of the sixteenth century, haphazardly preserved the memory of the ancients solely in outdoor contexts. Indeed, the Palazzo Nuovo constitutes a perfect, striking complex with a continuing alternation of wall divisions in plaster and travertine. Internally, Latin and Greek inscriptions and important reliefs decorate the walls.

The original "sky blue" color of the palace (recently restored), harmoniously synchronized with the terracotta pavement and wooden decorations of the wooden coffered ceilings and emphasized the marble material of the sculptures. The terracotta pavement was replaced in the nineteenth and twentieth centuries with large marble panels. Details of the ceiling, in part decorated with stucco and frescoes, were brought to light during the most recent work on the building. The architecture of the palace underwent noteworthy embellishments during the pontificate of Alexander VII (1655-1667) and Clement X (1670-1676). Clement X commissioned the wooden ceilings in the principal rooms. In the same years, the "Wool and Silk Guild," which played a very important cultural role, obtained permission to use the building. During this moment of concession, the inventory of the statues numbered 44. In 1698, when the "Agricultural Arts" obtained permission to use the building, the number of statues had increased to 50.

In 1733, Pope Clement XII inaugurated the new public collection of antiquity, organized according to the criteria of a modern museum. The pope made a great

Hall of the Doves

effort to purchase the sculptures that previously adorned the house of the Cardinal Alessandro Albani. Cardinal Albani had meticulously formed a collection of ancient masterpieces that originated in other collections and excavations. With the acquisition of the Albani Collection, consisting of 418 sculptures, and the following acquisitions and donations in 1745-1750, during the pontificate of Pope Benedict XIV, the collections became very prestigious. As a result, the rooms were arranged according to an itinerary, today substantially maintained, that also emphasized the documentary value of the sculptures. In order to restore the statues, many Roman sculptors were summoned. They reworked the surfaces, often mutilated, to pristine condition. Frequently, their interpretation of the statues was very learned. Between 1812 and 1818, the palace underwent many changes, and the statues housed in the Church of Santa Maria in Aracoeli were acquired.

In 1816, in order to increase the existing space, the first room on the right on the ground floor, called "The Inscription Hall" and the second small room, called "Hall of the Urn," were resystematized.

The museum contains works of ancient marble statues, displayed both according to an itinerary that follows typological criteria (e.g., Hall of the Emperors, Hall of the Philosophers) and also according to aesthetic principles that denote central sculptures as "masterpieces" (e.g., Hall of the Faun, Hall of the Gladiator). The collectors' predilection predominantly inspires the Gallery and the Great Hall on the first floor, through the ornamental (rather than typological) arrangement of the sculptures. This constitutes the first public collection of antiquity that became the model for very important collections housed in museums located throughout the world.

Lobby

The internal space of the ground floor is articulated according to the architectural concept that seventeenth century palaces borrowed from the ancient Roman *domus*. The portico, divided by openings and niches symmetrically arranged and framed by architraves and columns in travertine, contains statues of large dimensions and some masterpieces once part of the Belvedere Collection in the Vatican and later donated to the City of Rome. The covered vaults (part barrel and part arched) create a particular variation of light and offer a visual effect that culminates in the central part that leads to the internal courtyard. Above, large shell-shaped ornaments scenographically complete the decoration. Roman inscriptions, for the most part funerary, are inserted in the walls.

Statue of Minerva

The sculpture, of colossal dimensions (over three meters high), was previously located on the piazza at the base of the staircase of the Palazzo Senatorio and in the portico of the Palazzo dei Conservatori.

The deity is represented standing, with her weight resting on her right leg, and her left leg slightly bent. She wears a large chiton, with folds rendered with a flat chisel. Around her waist, a large belt holds the chiton in place. Holes, to which attachments in metal were added, are visible on the belt. Some holes for the attachment of parts consisting of different material are visible on the *apoptygma*, on the chest. The head and the arms are assembled according to the conception of large acroliths. The head, covered by a helmet, has hollow eye cavities originally filled with hard stones and metal. Therefore, the sculpture is a direct inspiration from the famous chryselephantine (in gold and ivory) statue that Pheidias created for the Athenian temple of the deity in the middle of the fifth century BC. Possibly, the statue was created by Greek craftsmanship in the second century BC for a very important temple.

The empress, the wife of
Antoninus Pius (138-161 AD),
appears in the guise of the
goddess Ceres, protectress of
agriculture. Her left hand tightly
holds a cornucopia. Recent
restoration of the statue has
revealed the remains of gilding on
her face and among the locks of
hair, and the remains of metal on
her chest, perhaps decorated with
a metal pectoral.

Fountain in the courtyard
with the "Marforio" statue

Courtyard

The middle of the lobby connects to the courtyard. The statue called "Marforio" overlooks
a fountain that is part of the scenographic wall enclosing the far end of the courtyard.
The statue is called Marforio because in the sixteenth century it was found in the Forum
of Mars (*Martis Forum*, the name that the ancients gave to the Forum of Augustus).
The statue, which is of colossal dimensions, has been known of since the sixteenth century
and in 1594 Bescapè added the typical attributes of Ocean to the colossal-scale statue.
Many scholars identify it as a representation of the Tiber or some other river divinity
that adorned a fountain in antiquity. Long hair, a beard, and a very thick moustache
characterize the tilted head of the figure reclining on his left side. Stylistically the piece
dates to the Flavian period (first century AD). During the Renaissance it enjoyed particular
notoriety because Romans affixed "pasquinate" to it. "Pasquinate" are defamatory
writings against the government that the people signed with the name Pasquino.

The two statues placed on either side of the fountain in niches and known as the Satyrs of the Valley were found in Rome near the Theater of Pompey. They were preserved for a long period of time not far from where they were discovered, i.e., in the courtyard of the Palazzo della Valle. These two mirroring statues that depict Pan, the Greek god of the countryside and nature, are linked to the cult of Dionysus. This divinity, half-man and half-goat with a bearded face and ferine horns, is also defined unequivocally by the panther skin draped over the chest. Each Capitoline image preserves a statue in high relief depicting a figure with an upraised arm that sticks out, holding a basket full of bunches of grapes balanced on its head.

They have been considered decorations of the Theater of Pompey and utilized as Telamones, statues used as architectural structures of support. The fine modeling of the surfaces and the excellent workmanship suggest that they are works of the late Hellenistic period, and possibly were placed either in a small portico or a loggia connected to the area of the theater.

Group of Polyphemus

The group represents Polyphemus who grips a young boy lying at his feet. The work, missing the right arm of the Cyclops and the head of the small boy, comes from the Vatican Collections. In 1636, the Conservators inscribed the date of the piece's acquisition on the base. At this time, both the arm with the syrinx and the head were added according to the hypothesis that the two figures were "Pan and a small boy." Polyphemus is nude, seated on a rock with a ferine skin draped on his thigh. A third eye characterizes his face, a distinctive feature of the Cyclops, the son of the god of the sea, Poseidon. The group illustrates one of the most salient moments from the *Odyssey*, when Ulysses and his companions find themselves in the cave of Polyphemus. This group (dating to the late Imperial period), possibly pertains to the Hellenistic archetype of Ulysses, who extends the cup to Polyphemus.

The colossal statue was found in two parts, torso and detached head, in the sixteenth century nearby the Forum of Nerva. Until the end of the eighteenth century, the statue was identified as Pyrrhus, the famous king of Epirus.
It is an image of Mars, represented standing, wearing a *lorica* (military breastplate that recalls the martial activity and ensuing peace of which the god was the guarantor). The decoration of the breastplate is very rich; it depicts the head of Medusa and two winged griffins flanking a candelabrum upheld by a palmette. Among many other decorations, the masks and pairs of elephant heads led to the identification of the statue as Pyrrhus. There are many noteworthy modern additions, including the shield, part of the helmet, and legs that appear squat and shortened (although they are adorned with impressive boots). The head of the god, with a rich beard, curly hair, and Corinthian helmet, suggests that the sculpture dates to the Flavian age (first century AD). Probably the statue was located outside the Temple of Mars Ultor and it is referable to the restoration of the simulacrum, damaged by a serious fire.

Pink Aswan granite crocodile,
from the Iseo Campense area

The Egyptian Collection

The first Capitoline collection of Egyptian antiquities was begun in the eighteenth
century with the acquisition of the statues of Villa Verospi Vitelleschi. As early as the
Middle Ages, the Obelisk of Ramses II was erected on the Capitoline Hill, and was
considered a polemical snub to the pope, who had had another obelisk placed in front
of the Rotunda of Sant'Andrea. From archival documents and images we can see how
Egyptian monuments were used to decorate the entrance to two Capitoline buildings as
early as the sixteenth century, and were exhibited for their symbolic and political nature.
The layout of the square devised by Michelangelo underscores cultural links with the
Egyptian world with the placing, in 1549, of the statues of the Nile and Tigris,
transformed into the Tiber, at the foot of the Palazzo Senatorio stairway. The Egyptian
lions, which are still extant, were placed at the foot of the Capitoline graded ramp in
1582. During the papacy of Clement XI (1700-1721), four statues found in the area of
Villa Verospi Vitelleschi (the ancient *Horti Sallustiani*) were bought, donated to and
housed in the Palazzo Nuovo. They had originally been in the Egyptian pavilion that
the Emperor Hadrian had built in the *horti*. The collection was augmented during the
eighteenth century when the statues of Ptolemy and Arsinoe were moved to the
courtyard of the Palazzo dei Conservatori, and in 1748 Pope Benedict XIV had the Hall
of the Canopus fitted out to contain sculptures from the Canopus of Hadrian's Villa and
the Sanctuary of Isis and Serapis in Campus Martius.
In 1838, however, almost all the Egyptian sculptures at the Capitoline were moved
to the Vatican. In 1907 the archaeologist Orazio Marucchi re-organized the small yet
prestigious nucleus (which is still part of the Capitoline collections) of Egyptian
artefacts that came to light during excavations undertaken after 1870 to modernise the
capital's urban structure and during excavations in the Iseo Campense area in 1883.
Unlike collections in other museums, this collection in the Palazzo Nuovo does not
include Egyptian finds brought in from Egypt, but only objects found within Rome
and relating to the city's monuments, a sign of just how important Egyptian culture was
to Ancient Rome.

Basanite sphinx of Pharaoh
Amasis II from the twenty-sixth
(Sais) dynasty (568-526 BC),
from the Iseo Campense area

Decorated bell-shaped crater
in dark grey granite,
from the Canopus
of Hadrian's Villa

Doghead of Nectanebo II
in grey granite,
from the Iseo Campense area

In the courtyard there are three grey granite columns, recovered in the Sanctuary of Isis and Serapis in Campus Martius. The relief frieze was inscribed around the shaft, as in the *columnae coelatae* (columns partially incorporated into the wall), and depicts, on each column, four pairs of priests standing on high footstools. Some are depicted making offerings to the deities, others as they hold aloft sacred objects.

The priests' heads are shaved and crowned with laurel leaves; they are wearing robes fastened under their arms, unlike the bearers of "Canopic" vases, who, according to ritual, wore tight-fitting robes and veils over their hands. These reliefs tell us much about how the Egyptian cult blended seamlessly into Roman religion. One of the most representative works is certainly the bell-shaped grey granite crater from the Canopus of Hadrian's Villa. The vase displays a frieze defined by the two handles in the form of feline protomes; a strip of cloth, knotted at its base and forming two fringes, flows from the neck of the felines. The frieze, in four scenes, depicts an offering to the deity and displays sacred symbols.

A series of animals personify the main Egyptian deities: the "Crocodile" in pink Aswan granite, from the Isis Temple (Iseo Campense) in Campus Martius, incarnated the deity of Sobek, one of the most important in the El-Faiyûm region; the two sculptures in grey granite of the "Dogheads," also found in the same sector of Campus Martius, are the incarnation of the Moon god Thoth, sitting on their haunches while their front legs are bent as if kneeling. The collection also contains an important Basanite sphinx on a rectangular plinth; the sphinx is perched on her outstretched haunches, her head aligned with her body. The sphinx is probably from a figurative class from the Ptolemaic period, which corresponds to the early Imperial period in Roman history.

Small ground floor rooms to the right

The "Small ground floor rooms" identify the three spaces on the ground floor
to the right of the lobby.
At the conclusion of the construction of the Palazzo Nuovo, every single space was
accessible to the portico. Only in the eighteenth-nineteenth centuries and following
periods were these rooms also designated as exhibition spaces. In particular, the
ground floor rooms on the right house very important epigraphic monuments.
Among these number the fragments of the post-Caesarian Roman calendars, all of
which record the new year that Caesar defined as 365 days, and the magistrate list
called "the Minor *Fasti*," in relation to the more famous *Fasti* housed in the Palazzo
dei Conservatori.
The first room houses many portraits of private Romans, among which one of the
most important is that related to a member of the Julio-Claudian family, maybe
Germanicus, son of Drusus the Elder, or Drusus the Elder himself (middle of the
first century AD).

Funerary urn
of Titus Statilius Aper

The altar-funerary urn, found on the Janiculum, was transported through the orders of Paul III to the Belvedere in the Vatican (1542). In 1743, Benedict XIV ordered its transfer to the Capitoline Museum.

The sepulchral monument, noteworthy for its dimensions and decoration, was sculpted on three sides. There is an unfinished cavity in the back, which must have contained vases for the ashes. Two inscriptions are engraved on the plinth. One records that two parents dedicate the altar to their son, *Titus Statilius Aper, mensor aedificiorum* – a sort of master builder – and to their daughter-in-law *Orcivia Anthis*. The other inscription is a metrical play on the last name *Aper*, which in Latin means boar, through reference to the boar hunted by the mythical Meleager. The instruments, which *Statilius* used in work, appear on both sides of the funerary urn. The portrait of his wife is located in a seashell at the center of the crowning. Stylistically and epigraphically, the tomb dates to the first century AD, when the dead predominantly were cremated.

In 1582, or a little before, a private citizen found this imposing sarcophagus outside Porta San Giovanni, between the Via Latina and Via Labicana, in a mausoleum known as "Mount of Grain." The sarcophagus, a *kline* (bed) type produced in Attica, is one of the largest of this kind ever found. All four sides are decorated. In the back, the decoration is in unfinished low relief, maybe because it was placed against a wall in the tomb. The deceased couple is represented in a reclining pose on the lid. The physiognomy of the faces dates the work to the second century AD. The sculptural narration centers on the figure of Achilles. On the frontal side, the youth brandishes a sword, freeing himself from his female dress. Ulysses discovered the Greek hero, hidden on Scyros among the daughters of Lycomedes, in order to avoid the Trojan War. On the sides of the scene sit king Agamemnon, on the right, and Lycomedes, on the left. The left side represents Achilles, who departs from Lycomedes. On the back, he prepares for his duel against Hector. On the right side, finally, Priam asks for the restitution of his deceased son's body.

Gallery of the Museum

The wide staircase joins the ground floor to the first floor of the museum. Reliefs belonging to sarcophagi of the late Imperial period are inserted on the back walls. Within the aedicules are sculptures. The head of the statue on the right is unrelated to the body, probably an original of the Hellenistic age. After the second ramp, one arrives in the Gallery of the Museum. The long Gallery, which extends the entire length of the Capitoline Museum, connects different exhibition rooms. It offers the visitor a variety of statue collections, portraits, reliefs, and inscriptions displayed by the eighteenth century Conservators in a casual manner. Indeed, they were more concerned with producing architectural symmetry and a general ornamental effect than accurate historical, artistic, and archaeological documentation. The overall effect is disorganized and inhomogeneous, but it preserves an exceptional example of the historical past. Inscriptions of small dimensions are inserted and framed on the walls. Among them is a consistent group originating from a common tomb (*columbarium*) of the freedmen and freedwomen of Livia. The sculptures are illustrated beginning with the left wall.

The sculpture was discovered during the reconstruction of the Church of Sant'Agnese. The sculptor Alessandro Algardi (1602-1654) conducted a complete restoration of the statue. He probably modified the ancient iconography of Hercules who domesticates the hind of Ceryneia to the iconography of Hercules who kills the Hydra. At any rate, the work is a Roman reworking (dating to the second century AD) of a Greek creation attributed to Lysippus (fourth century BC) who, according to sources, sculptured the labours of Hercules.

The torso constitutes the only ancient part of this prestigious and famous statue. It seems to be an optimal reworking of the Discobolos that Myron made in 460 BC. The interpretation of the statue as a wounded warrior in the moment of falling is the product of the reworking of the sculpture by Pierre-Étienne Monnot, who lived from 1658 to 1733.

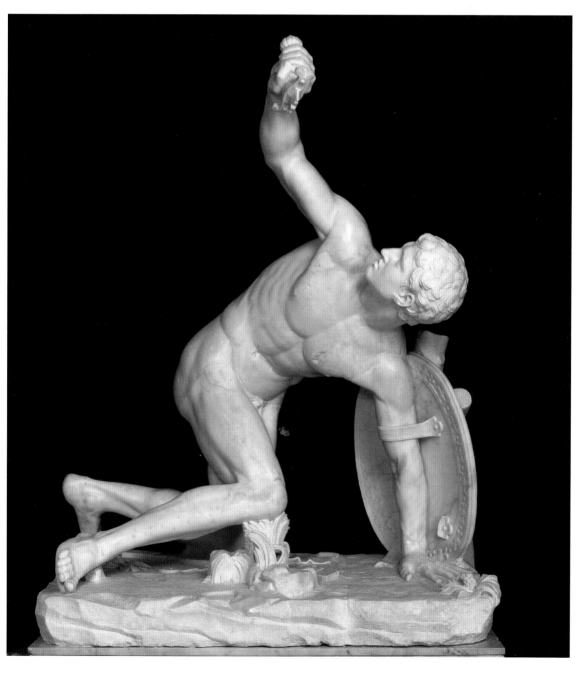

Statue of baby Hercules who strangles the snakes

The statuette represents a real baby, depicted as the little hero. It has been interpreted as a portrait of baby Caracalla, or, more recently, Annius Verus, the Emperor Marcus Aurelius' son.

Statue of Leda and the swan

This group is a sculptural representation of the erotic theme of Leda and Zeus in the guise of a swan. Leda, nude, is depicted in the act of lifting up her mantle with her left arm in order to protect the swan from the eagle in the act of snatching it. With her right hand, she holds the swan. The figure is leaning on a tree trunk placed to her right. The statue could be a reworking of a group attributed to the Greek Timotheos, in the fourth century BC, and very common in many replicas beginning in the first century BC.

This is one of the best Imperial age copies, derived from Lysippus' famous creation. It represents the youthful, winged god in the act of stringing the bow that he used to shoot his arrows of love.

MUNIFICENTIA · SS · D · N · BENEDICTI
PP · XIV · A · D · MDCCLIII

The *Tabula Iliaca*, detail

Hall of the Doves

The room on the right derives its name from the pavement mosaic found in 1737 in Hadrian's Villa in Tivoli. It is preserved, for the most part, in its eighteenth century phase. At that time, the room was called "Hall of the Miscellaneous Objects" because it contained works of typologically diverse material. All of the pieces belonged to the collection of Cardinal Alessandro Albani, the first acquisition of the Capitoline Museum.

Male and female portraits of private citizens, arranged at the time on shelves along the walls, are currently ordered in the same way, with the exception of some alterations. In 1817, the large marble crater with vegetal decorations located in the center of the room changed the name of the space to the "Hall of the Vase." Today the vase is located along the back wall of the Gallery of the Capitoline Museum. During the first half of the eighteenth century, numerous Roman sepulchral inscriptions were used to decorate the upper part of the walls of this room. The arrangement of the inscriptions has never been altered.

The finds visible in the glass display cases are recorded in the list of acquisitions of the eighteenth century. Most noteworthy among the pieces displayed are the following: bronze *tabula* (third century AD) recording the honorific title of patron that the guild of the *Fabri* of *Sentinum* (Sassoferrato, in the Marche Region) bestowed to *Coretius Fuscus*; the *Tabula Iliaca*, a fragment of a miniature plaque in low relief (first century BC) with scenes from Homer's *Iliad* accompanied by explicit inscriptions; a bronze inscription from the Aventine, recording a dedication of the Fourth Cohort of the *Vigiles* to Septimius Severus and the Imperial family in 203 AD; the Decree of Pompeius Strabo, which conceded particular privileges to some Spanish knights who fought on the side of the Romans at the battle of Asculum, during the Social War (90-89 BC); the *Senatusconsultum* regarding Asclepiades of Klazomenes and his allies, the oldest remains of a Senate decree in bronze (78 BC), almost entirely preserved. One reads on the decree the conferral of the title *amici populi Romani* to three Greek navarchs that had fought on the side of the Romans during the Social War, or, perhaps, the Sullan War (83-82 BC). The text is in Latin, with a Greek translation appearing on the lower part of the tablet. The Greek text permitted a reconstruction of the fragmentary Latin text.

The statue, located at the center of the room, depicts a girl who protects a dove from the attack of a snake by hiding the dove in the folds of the mantle covering her long tunic. The snake is the product of modern restoration. The statue is a Roman copy of a Hellenistic original. In the Hellenistic age attention to the aspects of daily life, in all its forms, developed. Typical of this genre is the representation of children, often depicted at play, as in this sculpture. In particular, the figurative motif of the young girl with the dove finds a possible antecedent in the reliefs of the Greek funerary stelae of the fifth and fourth centuries BC.

Mosaic of the Doves

The mosaic, which gives the room its name, was found in 1737, at the center of a pavement, in a room in Hadrian's Villa in Tivoli. The scene is composed of four doves, one of which drinks, balanced on the rim of a bronze bowl. A figure in relief seems to uphold the handle. An astragal pattern recalling architectural motifs decorates the frame. Nevertheless, the mosaic is not entirely preserved. The border decorated with a garland, which was part of the Albani Collection, was donated to Frederick of Saxony. Now, it is on display in the Augusteum in Dresda. The mosaic is a figured panel composed of very tiny polychromatic marble and glass *tesserae*, placed at the center of a Hadrianic-period room (*émblema*). This type of decoration, produced in the Roman period for rich clients, is distinct from the other kinds of mosaic pavement, thereby constituting its high worth. The *émblema* is a copy of the work of Sosos, active in Pergamon in the second century BC. We have other copies of this work, including the mosaic in the House of the Faun in Pompey, that differ in particular details. The mosaic from Hadrian's Villa (second century AD) is the closest to the original scheme. The high level of skill employed in its production creates a surprising pictorial effect.

In 1824, the mosaic was found in the vineyards of the Jesuits on the Aventine, in front of the Church of Santa Prisca, on the site of the baths constructed by Trajan Decius (249-251 AD). Pope Leo XII (1823-1829) acquired them and placed them in this room. The mosaic represents two masks leaning on a socle projecting out from two walls that meet at an angle, seen in perspective. Two flutes lean on one wall. Their shadows project onto the wall. The female mask depicts a woman with large eyes and wide-open mouth. A ribbon, knotted into a bow at the center of her brow, appears in her curly hair with long ringlets. The physiognomic features of the man are exaggerated and ridiculed. The mouth is enormous. The nose is large and squashed. The eyes bulge out, and the cheeks are wrinkled. On his head is a crown of ivy and berries, decoration associated with the cult of Dionysus, which was linked closely to the birth of the Greek theater. The masks belong to two "types" from New Comedy, which developed in the Hellenistic period: the young woman, often sad for her misfortunes and the slave, fearful and mocking.

The work, constructed with polychromatic marble tesserae by an artist attentive of perspective and the effect of light and shade, probably belonged to an *émblema* pavement in an Imperial building on the Aventine.

It is thought to date to the second century AD, maybe the Hadrianic period.

Statue of a drunken old woman

The sculpture, reassembled from many fragments and heavily restored, depicts an old woman tightly holding onto a wine vase. The work appears on the list of Hellenistic representations of personages devoted to vices and represented in their degraded level of daily life. The rendering of the veins and wrinkling of the skin is very realistic, with particular attention to the drapery, suggesting that this is a copy of a work executed in the third century BC at Smyrna by a Myron known for his *anus ebria*.

The Capitoline Venus,
detail

Cabinet of Venus

The small polygonal room located at three-quarter's length of the Gallery was
created in the first decades of the nineteenth century. It provides a striking setting,
typical of a fountain, for the famous Capitoline Venus statue.

Capitoline Venus

The sculpture, of slightly larger than life size dimensions, was found near the Basilica of San Vitale around 1667-1670. In 1752, Pope Benedict XIV acquired it and donated it to the Capitoline collections. It is one of the most famous statues of the museum and boasts a series of reproductions that are located in many other international collections. It is made of precious marble (probably Parian), and represents Venus-Aphrodite nude and in contemplation, coming out of her bath. She is depicted with her arms following the curving contours of her soft and fleshy small-boned body and covering her breasts and pubic area. The right leg is forward and bent, and the left is resting. The head is slightly tilted towards the left. The hairstyle is complicated. Part of the hair is pulled up, in the form of hoops, at the top of her head and tied to form a bow. Other locks touch her shoulders. The expression of the face seems absent, psychologically depicted by the small, languid eyes and the small, fleshy mouth. The Capitoline Venus defines the so-called "Capitoline type," of which today one hundred replicas are known. It may be the variation of the Pudica Venus type. Scholars have debated at length regarding the chronology of the image of the deity and the chronology of the copies. The Capitoline Venus could be one of the first and most faithful replicas. Like all of the other depictions of this type, it was destined to decorate an Imperial complex of noteworthy sophistication.

Hall of the Emperors

From the opening of the museum to the public in 1734, the curators of the artistic
collections displayed in this room in the Capitoline Museum all of the busts, herms,
and portraits depicting Roman emperors, and personages of the Imperial circle.
The works on display are the product of a reasoned selection from the collection
during the nineteenth century, eventually reduced and rearranged according to
more rigorous and consequential historical and logical-thematic criteria. Today in
the Hall of the Emperors, 67 busts and portraits are on display, and in the center
is a seated statue of a woman. Eight ancient reliefs and a modern, honorary
inscription adorn the walls.
The busts, arranged for the most part in a double row on marble shelves, allow the
visitor to follow chronologically the development of Roman portraiture from the
Republican period to the late-antique period by offering quantitatively and, more
importantly, qualitatively rich illustrations.
The itinerary winds along in a helicoidal fashion in a clockwise direction.
Entering from the Hall of the Philosophers, the itinerary starts from the upper shelf
immediately to the left, and it terminates at the end of the lower shelf, immediately
to the right of the same entrance. The collection includes two portraits of Augustus.
The first is related to the moment immediately following his victorious battle of

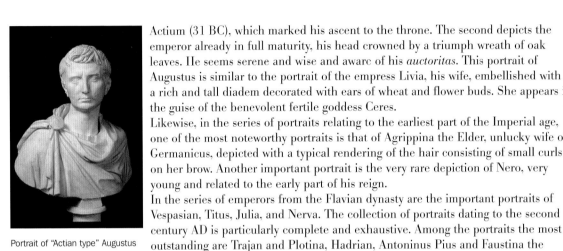

Portrait of "Actian type" Augustus

Portrait of Agrippina the Elder

Actium (31 BC), which marked his ascent to the throne. The second depicts the emperor already in full maturity, his head crowned by a triumph wreath of oak leaves. He seems serene and wise and aware of his *auctoritas*. This portrait of Augustus is similar to the portrait of the empress Livia, his wife, embellished with a rich and tall diadem decorated with ears of wheat and flower buds. She appears in the guise of the benevolent fertile goddess Ceres.

Likewise, in the series of portraits relating to the earliest part of the Imperial age, one of the most noteworthy portraits is that of Agrippina the Elder, unlucky wife of Germanicus, depicted with a typical rendering of the hair consisting of small curls on her brow. Another important portrait is the very rare depiction of Nero, very young and related to the early part of his reign.

In the series of emperors from the Flavian dynasty are the important portraits of Vespasian, Titus, Julia, and Nerva. The collection of portraits dating to the second century AD is particularly complete and exhaustive. Among the portraits the most outstanding are Trajan and Plotina, Hadrian, Antoninus Pius and Faustina the Elder, Marcus Aurelius and Faustina the Younger, Lucius Verus, and Commodus. In the male series of the emperors, one can follow the evolution of the hair and beard style. In the beginning the faces were clean-shaven, and later, the beard was worn long, "in Greek fashion," with the intent of appearing inspired and philosophically committed. In the female series, one can follow the development of hairstyles, from the tall, stacked, "scaffolded" hairstyles typical of the Flavian tradition, to those characterized by a ring-shaped bun (of varying size), typical of the entire Antonine period.

The Severan household (193-217 AD) is also well represented. It includes the portraits of the following: Septimius Severus, placed on an imposing bust of green alabaster, Julia Domna, his wife, and his children Geta and Caracalla. In addition, there are portraits of Elagabalus, Maximinus of Thrace, Trajan Decius, Aurelius Probus, and Diocletian.

The Imperial series ends with the head of the young Honorius (384-423 AD), the youngest child of the Emperor Theodosius, in prelude to the figurative modes of Byzantine art. The room contains numerous female portraits, with complicated hairstyles and, in some cases, wigs with very elaborate curls. Among these the most outstanding are the portrait of Faustina the Elder (wife of Antoninus Pius) and Faustina the Younger, who changed her hairstyle every time she gave birth to a child.

Eight different hairstyles of Faustina the Younger are known. The portrait of "the Flavian woman," who has a complex and articulated hairstyle and sophisticated facial features, is very prestigious. The polychromatic bust of a Roman woman, whose portrait comes from Smyrna and dates to the period of Alexander Severus, is unique. It was constructed out of distinct pieces, with the separate insertion of hair, like many other busts of this type belonging to this period. The hair, maybe lost, was restored in modern times with *nero antico* marble.

Hall of the Philosophers

Beginning with the foundation of the Capitoline Museum, this room, located next to the Hall of the Emperors, was created to house and display the portraits, busts, and herms depicting poets, philosophers, and orators from ancient Greece of the Classical and Hellenistic periods. In the Roman age, these portraits (according to the vogue introduced by the erudite Asinius Pollio in the second half of the first century BC) decorated public and private libraries, houses of the nobles, villas and parks of wealthy, sensitive connoisseurs of arts and philosophy.
Renaissance collectors embellished their palaces and their collections with the most representative images of many illustrious men.
Currently the Hall of the Philosophers displays 79 portraits. The identity of many portraits has been ascertained. Many portraits certainly are "reconstructions," i.e., created long after the death of the individual, and therefore only vaguely resemble the real physiognomic features. Others, instead, beginning in the Hellenistic period, reproduce, with great accuracy, the different physiognomies.
The collection begins with a numerous representation of herms depicting Homer, the most famous poet in antiquity. He is depicted conventionally as an old man, with a thick beard and hair. His eyes are already lifeless, corresponding not only to his legendary blindness but also the profound sensitivity and awareness of the soul and the destiny of man. The prototype of this portrait can be attributed to an artistic Rhodian school and can be dated close to 200 BC.

The portrait of Pindar, another famous Greek poet, is a reconstruction. Its statuary prototype dates back to an artistic moment influenced by the Severe style (first half of the fifth century BC).

The portrait identified as Pythagoras, the famous philosopher and mathematician of Samos, is interesting. A flat turban wrapped around his head characterizes this portrait. Socrates is depicted according to the portrait created by Lysippus around the middle of the fourth century BC, about half a century after the death of the philosopher. He is almost depicted as a satyr, with an upward turned, fleshy nose, round and protruding eyes, rounded brow, and wide mouth with swollen lips.

In addition, there are portraits depicting the three most famous Athenian tragic poets. The features of the face of Aeschylus are full and defined, decorated by a stylized and ornamental beard, maybe deriving from a prototype of about the middle of the fifth century BC. Sophocles has a squared and solid head. His beard and hair have short, rich locks, tied by a ribbon. Euripides is depicted as a man in his mature years, with a receding hairline and long hair that covers his ears. The prototype, which can be dated to 320 BC, preserves the traces of Lysippan style. Among the many portraits of famous individuals from the Greek world, many original portraits from the Roman period are displayed in this room. The bust of Cicero, famous statesman and man of letters, is depicted in his early 50s, at the peak of his intellectual and political powers. The general conception of this portrait is based on Greek portraiture during the late Hellenistic era. However, realistic features that belong to the more authentic Roman portraiture of the Republican age are clearly evident.

Herm of Homer
Herm of Pythagoras
Herm of Euripides
Bust of Cicero

Great Hall

Because of its ample, monumental size, this room constitutes the most
representative space of the entire Capitoline Museum complex.
The "Large hall in the middle" was decorated and designed to create harmony
between the exhibition space and the displayed statues. The four walls are divided
into vertical sections. In these sections, the cadence of the architectural order
evenly distributes the studied division of the room. The large seventeenth century
coffers on the ceiling harmonize with the walls. The diversity of the geometric
forms of the coffers, composed of octagonal, rectangular, and other shapes,
expresses the magnificence typical of the Baroque style. The engraving on the
rosettes, variously carved, enhances the richness of the ceiling. The crest of Pope
Innocent X Pamphilj, who was responsible for the completion of the palace, is
located in the center of the ceiling. Recent restoration has recuperated the colors
of the surfaces by emphasizing the richness of the composition.
A large door located on the long wall adjoining the Gallery is especially interesting.
In the first half of the eighteenth century, Filippo Barigioni designed the portal as
an arch with two winged Victories of very high quality.

The hunter with the hare

In 1747, the statue was found near Porta Latina. It depicts a nude youth that shows his prey, a hare. He leans on the spear held in his left hand. Altogether, this work represents a *pastiche* of the third century AD. The portrait depicts a personage of the second century AD, according to its similarity to works dating to the rule of Gallienus. Instead, the body depends on a Greek original dating to the middle of the fifth century BC, representing Perseus in the act of lifting up the head of Medusa.

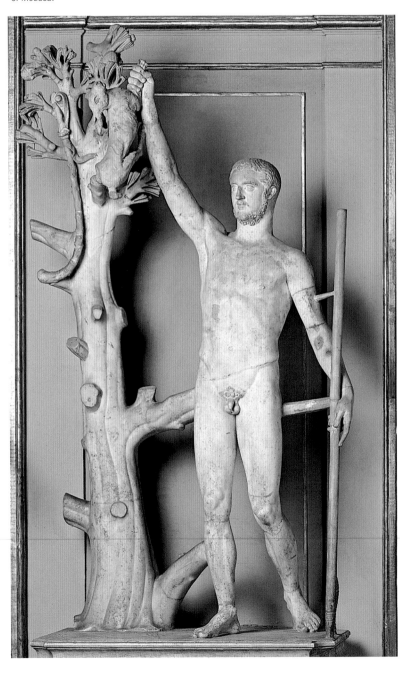

In 1734, Clement XII purchased the statue for the sum of 1000 *scudi* from the Duke of Palombara. The statue is a Roman copy of a reworking of the Apollo *Lykeios*, depicted with a lyre, by Praxiteles. Two sources testify that the original statue was located in Athens. First, the statue is depicted on some coins, and second, a brief note by the poet Lucian, who does not mention the author of the work, depicts the deity with a bow, at rest after a long exertion. This statue type was the object of many reworkings, until the late Hellenistic period. The lyre resting on the tripod acting as a support substitutes the bow. The god does not seem tired, resting after a heavy exertion. Rather, he seems concentrated in a moment of inspiration. In this work the psychological element that appears is in contrast to the other reposing statue, which conveys the feelings of tiredness. It is not possible to attribute it to Praxiteles or to his children. It is probably a later variant, ascribable to the Attic sculptor, Timarchides, who lived in the first half of the second century BC.

The Apollo of the *Omphalos* is thus named because one of the best preserved copies in the Museum of Athens depicts the *omphalós*. The *omphalós* is a rock venerated in Delphi. The Capitoline statue, originating from the Albani Collection, is a well made Roman copy of the Greek original attributed to Kalamis (470-460 BC). Some scholars identify it as the Apollo *Alexíkakos*, who wards off evil, vowed at Athens for the healing after the pestilence of 430-427 BC. Others identify it as the prototype of the Apollo sculpted by Onathas (490-460 BC).

Three elements of the statue indicate that it was created in the period of time between the end of the Severe style and beginning of the Classical style. They are the anatomical structure, rendered with the essential masses, the face of god, which has a benevolent expression, and the hairstyle "tightly braided" around the head.

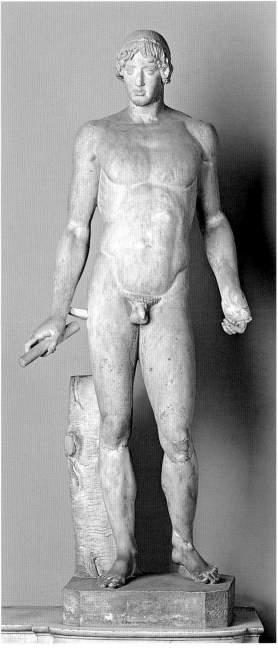

Harpocrates

In 1741, the statue was found in a room in the substructures of the "Pecile" in Hadrian's Villa. In 1744 Benedict XIV donated it to the Capitoline collections.

The god, son of Isis and Osiris, is represented nude, without pubic hair. The body type is soft and fleshy. He leans his weight on his right leg. Behind it, up to the height of the knee, is the representation of a palm trunk covered in fruit. The left leg is slightly bent and placed slightly back. The pelvic line is just visible, and the stomach is round and slightly prominent. The buttocks, round and well defined, underline the young age of the god. The right arm, just moved ahead, is bent. The hand rests at the height of his right nipple, and his index finger is raised and attached to his chin by a small strut. The arm is placed so that the finger brushes the lower lip, in the habitual gesture of silence. In the Roman period this gesture was interpreted as mystic, intended to insure the secrets of the religion. The left arm, held away from the body by a strut located at the height of the hips, extends ahead and bends. The left hand tightly holds a horn in its well-modeled fingers. The head, of refined workmanship, tilts to the left, in order to underline the particular expression of the child. The locks of hair, rendered with delicate carving, rest above the brow, to form short bangs. The hair is pulled up and held in place with a ribbon. This tuft of gathered hair supports a smooth hat, called the *pschent* (the motif representing the crown of Lower and Middle Egypt). Competent use of the drill in the hair and irises, depicted through the depression in the eyeball, suggests that the sculpture dates to the Hadrianic period. Perhaps the iconography of the figure is similar to an Alexandrine original, derived from a Praxitelean work, also known through numerous miniature bronze statuettes.

This statue is also known as the "Sosikles' type" because of the signature present on this important replica. The statue belonged to the Albani Collection. It is larger than life size and generally is attributed to the work of Polyclitus. Napolioni, instructor of Cavaceppi, restored the work. The right arm is raised, possibly originally holding a spear, on which the figure leaned. The head is turned toward the right leg, whereas the left arm holds up the hem of the drapery to reveal her wound.

Centaurs

Located in the center of the room, the two statues were found in Hadrian's Villa in Tivoli during Cardinal Furietti's excavation. In 1765, Clement XIII acquired the statues for the Capitoline Museum. Aristeas and Papias, artists from Aphrodisias, a city in Asia Minor, signed the sculptures, made of *bigio morato* marble. Aphrodisias had a school of skillful copyists of Greek works. In the last decades of the first century AD, some of these artists moved to Rome, where the munificence of the emperors and private citizens provided continual, well-rewarded work.

The majority of the most known sculptures, including the Centaurs of the Capitoline, date to the rule of Hadrian (second century AD). These statues are very famous due to the great skill and the rarity of the material, a prized marble extracted from the quarries on the promontory of Cape Tenaros in Lakonia. Anatomic details and distinction in the depiction of the features of the faces help characterize the age and emotions of the Centaurs. The young Centaur is happy and joyful. The old Centaur is old and suffering. The attempt to render the hair, beard, and tails with a metallic effect is evident and suggests that the statues derive from original ones constructed in bronze.

The *Lex de imperio Vespasiani* in the Hall of the Faun

Hall of the Faun

The hall acquired this name in 1817, when the statue of the Faun was placed in the center of the room. Inscriptions inserted in the eighteenth century cover the walls, divided into groups according to their content. One section is devoted to brickstamps. On the right wall, the *Lex de imperio Vespasiani* (first century AD) stands out among the epigraphic texts. This decree confers special power to the Emperor Vespasian. This precious document, recorded from the fourteenth century on the Capitoline Hill, is constructed of bronze with a particular technique. The text is not engraved but written when the metal was still hot.

Drunken faun
in rosso antico marble

The sculpture was discovered in 1736. Clemente Bianchi and Bartolomeo Cavaceppi were entrusted with the delicate and arduous restoration. They added many pieces of *rosso granato* marble, characterized by obvious grayish veins. They did not particularly modify the structure or the ancient image. As early as 1746, when it was purchased for the Capitoline collections, the sculpture aroused the admiration of travelers and cataloguers of the museum. The figure leans on his right leg. The left leg, which conforms to the original, is slightly forward and shows the foot rotated outward, indicating the rhythm of the dance. The idea of movement is deftly transmitted both through the slight rotation to the right and the musculature, with evident contraction along the back and buttocks on oblique planes, at the center of which there is a ponytail resting on the left buttock. The upper part of the torso, decorated by a *nebrís* (faun skin) knotted on the right shoulder, is characterized by masses of muscle well defined and by the impression of the ribs. The face, framed by long sideburns divided into locks, has protruding cheekbones. The half-opened mouth forms a smile, revealing a row of teeth. The empty eye sockets probably were filled with metals or hard stones. One of the fauns' properties was that of inseminating flocks and defending them from wolves. They were associated with abundant harvests and were, in many cases, represented by overflowing cornucopias. These creatures, connected with the cult of Dionysus, were probably part of the god's procession and are depicted dancing in a state of drunkenness, according to the iconography of the jovial and drunken friend of Dionysus. This, in fact, is closer to a human image and quite different from the creatures' long-forgotten demonic origins. Perhaps, this type was utilized in the decorative context of *horti*, exactly coinciding with the exaltation of bucolic motifs. It was a common statue type in the Roman period that reproduced themes from the late Hellenistic period, i.e., the late second century BC.

Hall of the Gladiator

This hall takes its name from the central sculpture, the Capitoline Gaul, wrongly
thought, at the time of its purchase by Alessandro Capponi, the then president of
the Capitoline Museum, to be a gladiator falling onto his own shield. It nonetheless
became the most famous work in the collections, and was often reproduced in
etchings and drawings.
The Gaul is surrounded by other high-quality copies: the Wounded Amazon, the
Hermes and Resting Satyr statues, while, next to the window, there is the delightful
Rococo group of Love and Psyche symbolising the poignant union of human soul
and divine love, in keeping with a theme that goes right back to Platonic
philosophy and that was a popular artistic theme from the earliest Hellenistic
period.

Generally, the sculpture is identified as the wounded Amazon type based on Pheidias' statue of the same subject. It is thought that Pheidias reutilized the theme of the conquered Amazon, dear to the Athenian culture of the fifth century BC. The delicate and luminescent rendering of the drapery is similar to the Amazons depicted on the frieze of the Parthenon. The support is on the right leg, and the right arm is raised to hold a bow. The statue comes from Villa d'Este (located inside the ancient perimeter of Hadrian's Villa). In 1753 Pope Benedict XIV donated it to the Capitoline collections. Interpretation of the type is difficult because of consistent restorations. Indeed, Bartolomeo Cavaceppi (responsible for a great number of eighteenth century interpolations) almost completely replicated the motif of the wounded Amazon.

In 1753 Pope Benedict XIV donated the statue to the Capitoline Museum. After the Treaty of Tolentino, it was handed over to the French. It was returned to the Capitoline collections in 1815.

The sculpture represents a young Satyr, recognizable by his particularly pointed ferine ears.

In a relaxed pose of abandonment he rests his right elbow on a tree trunk. The entire figure is arranged on an oblique plane.

It is inclined on one side, according to the typical "Praxitelean" pose, with a branch acting as a strut. The right hand tightly holds a flute, and the right leg is bent and slightly positioned back. The left leg is straight, with the foot acting as a support. The left leg is counter-balanced by the arm held away from the body and the forearm rotated behind with the back of the hand resting on the left hip. The panther skin is arranged obliquely from the right shoulder to the left hip. It also falls on the shoulders and back with rich folds formed by the knot placed at the height of the hip.

Recent restoration revealed consistent remains of a yellow patina on the locks of hair, possible preparation for gilding. The sculpture is considered unanimously a copy of Praxiteles' *Anapauómenos* ("resting") Satyr, reproduced in numerous copies during the Roman period. They were utilized as villa decorations in small groves and fountains.

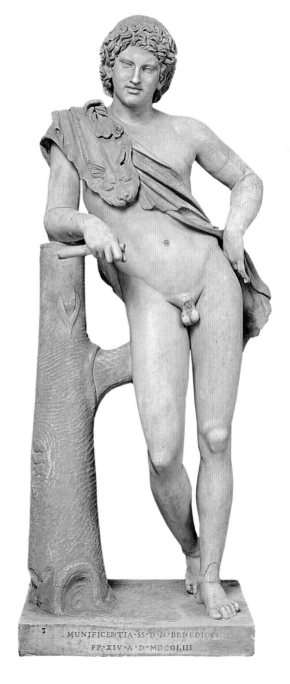

7   MUNIFICENTIA·SS·D·N·BENEDICTI
FP·XIV·A·D·MDCCLIII

Albani Hermes-Antinous

The statue appears in the inventory of the Cardinal Albani in 1733 as "Antinous from Hadrian's Villa." Pope Clement XII acquired it for the recently constructed museum. Recent restoration revealed that the reinsertion of the head, which accompanies the rhythm of the body, was executed with extreme care. The head inclines downward and is slightly rotated toward the right. The torsion of the neck and the tilt of the head with downward gaze are common of the iconography of Antinous. Therefore, if it is not possible to catalogue the sculpture precisely as the youth deified after his tragic death, it is possible to hypothesize that the physiognomic features of the youth are similar to the representation of a divinity. The statue's provenience from Hadrian's Villa suggests that the emperor himself, a refined collector, commissioned the work to skillful artisans. These sculptors were active in Rome, and their products were clear interpretations of classical works. Understanding of this sculpture is unsure because of the absence of qualifying attributes, the changed position of the arms, and the coexistence of themes and elements typical of the cultural syncretism of this period. These features also obscure the hand of the great author, whom many scholars identify as Praxiteles, Euphranor, or Polyclitus. In fact, a recent study recognizes the similarity between this sculpture and a bronze statuette representing Hermes (preserved in Paris at the Petit Palais), a Roman era replica of an original by Polyclitus ascribable to the first works of the Argive master.

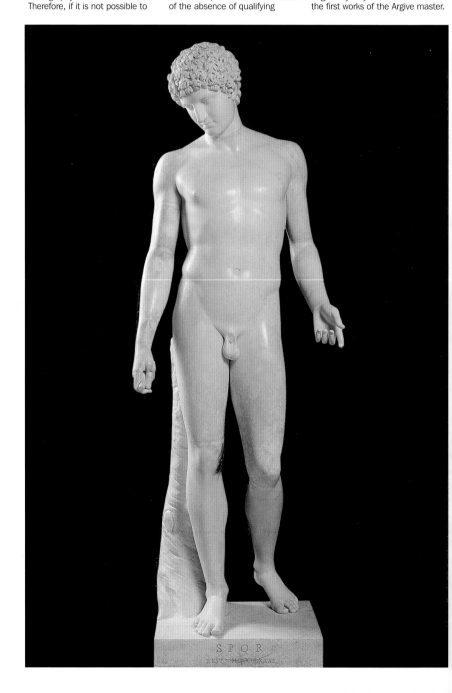

The sculpture, reproduced several times in engravings and drawings, is perhaps the most famous sculpture of the entire collection. In 1734, the statue was acquired from the Ludovisi Sculpture Collection. Probably the Ludovisi family found the statue on the premises of their villa. The Villa Ludovisi was situated on the ancient *horti* of Caesar, which through inheritance then passed into the possession of the historian Sallustius.

With great pathos the statue depicts a wounded Gaul (Galatian). His attributes are very evident: shield, *torques* around his neck, complete nudity, disordered locks of hair and moustache. The very visible wound indicates the sculptor's intention to depict the warrior in the last moment of resistance to his pain. Perhaps the image pertains to the great donation created during the era of Pergamon that Attalus placed along the terrace of the Temple of *Athena Nikephóros* in order to celebrate his victories over the Galatians. It is possible that the Ludovisi statue group (today located in the Palazzo Altemps) also belongs to Attalus' donation. Scholars do not agree on the date of this splendid sculpture. A recent hypothesis dates this copy to the Caesarian age. Another hypothesis asserts that the statue is a direct copy or the Pergamene original.

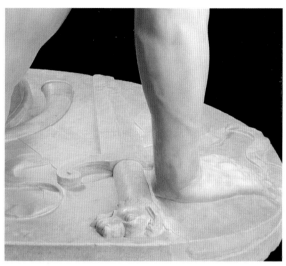

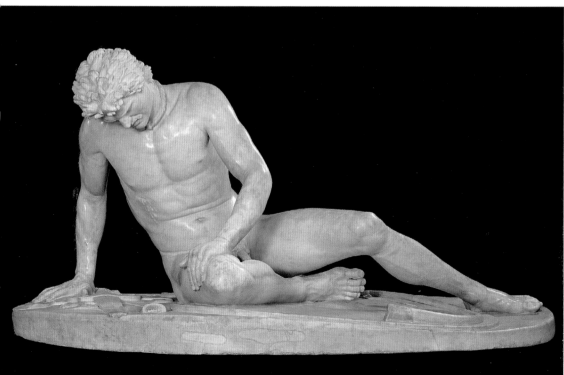

A fragment of the colossal
statue of Constantine
in the courtyard
of the Palazzo dei Conservatori

Palazzo dei Conservatori

At least by 1363, the public statutes entrusted the seat of the public magistracy to
the Conservators. Their task was to assist the Senator in the governing of the city.
By the fourteenth century, the site had been occupied by the Palace of the
Banderesi, captains of the public *militia* organized in "the satisfactory partnership
between crossbowmen and marines." Around the middle of the fifteenth century,
Pope Nicholas V commissioned the construction of the palazzo ("*is summus pontifex*
[...] *aliud (palatium) Conservatorum a fundamentis construi* [...] *facit*").
Images illustrating the Capitoline palaces before the transformation engineered
by Michelangelo show a building with a long portico with arches and columns that
houses the premises of arts and trade gilds. A continuous series of cross-windows
distinguished the upper part of the façade. The windows provided light to the main
rooms of the noble floor. Two loggias with double lancet windows facing the piazza
were located on the far ends of the palace. Also a loggia with three arches
delineated the façade facing the Campus Martius.
The courtyard, accessible through the portico on the piazza, was smaller than the
current one. (A document attests to the enlargement that took place in 1522).
On the right side, a series of ogival arcades characterized the courtyard.
The arcades were adjacent to another space, first site of the Capitoline "statue
collection." A staircase composed of a single flight led to the upper floor.
In 1563, Michelangelo began work, transforming the ancient palace, still in its
mediaeval phase, into a building of the classical nobility, according to a "language"
developed during his long experience with Roman architecture. He completely
changed the façade, locking it into a geometric scheme of two orders: Corinthian,
with gigantic pilasters that extend and divide the entire structure, and Ionic, with
columns that support the vaults of the portico. Michelangelo proposed the same
scheme of the façade for the courtyard, on the side corresponding to the entrance.
However, in this case, he emphasized the division of the two orders. According to
an ancient drawing, he arranged the Consular and Triumphal *Fasti*, found in 1546
in the Roman Forum, on the far wall. The transformation of the monumental
staircase and the new arrangement of the Conservators' Apartment effected the
interior of the palace so much that the early sixteenth century cycle of frescoes
that decorated the rooms facing the piazza was lost.
Under the pontificate of Clement XI (1720), Alessandro Specchi was the last person
to change the courtyard. He systematized the back wall that had been stripped of
the ancient *Fasti* fragments already for some time (1586) and transferred to a room
on the upper floor. Specchi, following the architectural drawing of Michelangelo,
deepened the portico to create a monumental space to house the precious ancient
sculptures just purchased from the Cesi Collection, i.e., the seated goddess Roma
and the colossal Barbarian figures made of *bigio morato* marble.

The courtyard of the Palazzo
dei Conservatori with the reliefs
depicting Provinces and trophies
of arms from the Temple
of Hadrian in Piazza di Pietra
and fragments from the acrolith
of Constantine

Courtyard

On the right side of the courtyard of the the Palazzo dei Conservatori are the remnants
of the ogival arches that gave access to the room housing the "statue collection."
From the beginning of Capitoline collections of antiquity, the courtyard has always
represented the privileged location as a sort of attraction for the appropriation and
preservation of the past. The works of art that gradually came to the palace were
tokens of the cultural continuity left by the ancient world, a virtual bridge to a glorious
past. The fragments of the colossal marble statue of Constantine are located on the
right side of the courtyard. These are different parts – head, hands, feet, and part of the
arms – of the large statue of the emperor. They were discovered in 1486 under the
pontificate of Innocent VIII in the western apse of the Basilica of Maxentius, finished
by Constantine, in the Roman Forum. The statue represented the emperor seated on a
throne, according to a model relating to statues of Jupiter. It was constructed according
to the acrolithic technique; marble composed only the nude parts of the body, whereas
drapery of gilded bronze or even of stucco covering a supporting structure composed
the other parts. The head, of imposing size, depicts the sharply marked facial features.
The work dates between 313, the year of Constantine's dedication of the Basilica, and
324, when the portrait of the emperor began to appear with the diadem, the traces of
which are visible on the marble. The reliefs of the Provinces and trophies of arms,
originating in the Temple of Hadrian in the Piazza di Pietra are on the left side of the
courtyard. Some of the reliefs, counter-marked with the crests of the Conservators,

The colossal statue also depicts a Dacian prisoner, with two different types of marble: *pavonazzetto* marble, with vivid purple veins, is used for the drape-covered parts, while a white marble is used for the hands and head. The very intense facial features communicate self-possessed melancholy, and very successfully convey the feelings of the vanquished. The work was originally part of the decorations for Trajan's Forum, and comes from Villa Borghese.

Also from Trajan's Forum, albeit a decorative statue from Constantine's Arch, is the fragment of the statue of Dace, which belongs to the same series and is now placed alongside it. It was removed from Constantine's Arch in 1733 during Clement XII's papacy and placed in the Capitoline Museums

were found at the end of the sixteenth century, whereas, others were found in the same area, beginning in 1883. The reliefs were located in the temple that Antoninus Pius dedicated in 145 AD to his predecessor and foster father Hadrian, who was deified upon death. The series of reliefs represents the personifications of different provinces subject to the Roman Empire, recognizable by specific attributes. Indeed, one of the characteristics of Hadrian's reign was his attention given to the relationships with the various Provinces. This aspect brought him on long travels through the boundless extension of the Roman Empire. Incorporated into the Palazzo della Borsa, the entire right side of the temple, with eleven channeled columns capped by massive Corinthian capitals, is preserved in the Piazza di Pietra. The statuary group composed of the seated statue of Roma and the two Prisoners in *bigio morato* marble is located on the far side of the courtyard inside the portico built by Alessandro Specchi. In 1720, Clement XI acquired the statuary group from the Cesi Collection. The group, already arranged in this form, was reproduced in ancient engravings when it was located in the garden of the Cesi household, in the Borgo. The central figure, representing a seated divinity derived from a model of the Pheidian circle, was transformed into Roma with the addition of typical attributes of this personification. The statue was placed on a base decorated on the frontal part by a relief depicting a subjugated province, probably originally part of the decoration of an arch dating to the first century AD. The two colossal Barbarian figures, whose heads were added in the modern period, are particularly precious because they are made of rare *bigio* marble. They are comparable to the series of Dacian prisoners created for the decoration of Trajan's Forum.

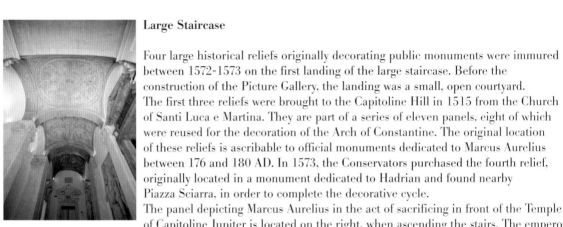

The marvellous stucco vaults
over the Large Staircase

Large Staircase

Four large historical reliefs originally decorating public monuments were immured
between 1572-1573 on the first landing of the large staircase. Before the
construction of the Picture Gallery, the landing was a small, open courtyard.
The first three reliefs were brought to the Capitoline Hill in 1515 from the Church
of Santi Luca e Martina. They are part of a series of eleven panels, eight of which
were reused for the decoration of the Arch of Constantine. The original location
of these reliefs is ascribable to official monuments dedicated to Marcus Aurelius
between 176 and 180 AD. In 1573, the Conservators purchased the fourth relief,
originally located in a monument dedicated to Hadrian and found nearby
Piazza Sciarra, in order to complete the decorative cycle.
The panel depicting Marcus Aurelius in the act of sacrificing in front of the Temple
of Capitoline Jupiter is located on the right, when ascending the stairs. The emperor
is depicted with a veiled head, pouring incense on a tripod. Next to him stand the
camillus, young assistant for sacrifices, a *flamen*, recognizable by his characteristic
hat, and a *victimarius*, ready to sacrifice a bull that appears behind the group.
The scene takes place before the Temple of Capitoline Jupiter. This is one of the
most detailed depictions of the temple, even though it appears with four Corinthian
columns instead of six due to spatial limitations. The Capitoline triad appears in the
pediment and a quadriga is located on the peak of the roof.
The second relief represents a triumphal parade. The emperor, wearing a toga and
guiding a chariot led by four horses, is on the verge of passing through a triumphal
arch. A lictor and a flutist (*tibicen*) precede him. Behind, a small winged Victory
crowns the victorious general.
The relief depicting Imperial clemency is located on the same wall. Riding a horse,
Marcus Aurelius is dressed in military garb with a breastplate and *paludamentum*.
He holds up his right hand, on the verge of bestowing his clemency on two
barbarians kneeling in front of him in a gesture of submission. The pose of the
emperor is very similar to the pose of the large bronze statue located in the piazza,
although in the statue in the piazza Marcus Aurelius is depicted in civilian dress. The
fourth panel, originating in a monument built to honor Hadrian, depicts the emperor
entering the city (*adventus*), welcomed by the Genius of the Senate, the Genius of
the People of Rome, and the goddess Roma. The deity is characterized by a short
tunic, which reveals her right shoulder, and a plumed helmet covering her head.
Two other large historical reliefs, remnants from the demolition of the so-called
"Arco di Portogallo," and transferred to the Capitoline Hill in 1664, decorate the
other landings of the monumental staircase. The Arco di Portogallo, located on
the Via Lata (the current Via del Corso), derived its name from its vicinity to the
Portuguese Embassy. It was a late-antique monument completely decorated with
reused material. It was destroyed in 1662 under the pontificate of Alexander VII
in order to enlarge the road.

Relief from a monument constructed in honor of Marcus Aurelius: the emperor makes a sacrifice in front of the Temple of Capitoline Jupiter

Relief from a monument constructed in honor of Marcus Aurelius: the triumph of the emperor

The two Capitoline panels, originating in a monument in honor of Hadrian, probably represent the only surviving elements of the decoration of the lost arch. The first panel represents the Emperor Hadrian presiding over a ceremony linked with the distribution of food to Roman children.

The emperor is depicted on a high podium. The figures of the Genius of the Senate and Genius of the People of Rome stand below him, in front of the podium. In the foreground stands a child wearing a toga. On the possible occasion of the reuse of the relief, the faces of the figures underwent important recarving in order to be adapted to the new monument.

The second of the historical reliefs taken from the Arco di Portogallo was arranged on the landing of the large staircase that leads to the Picture Gallery. It represents the apotheosis of Sabina. Although unloved by her husband, the Emperor Hadrian, she became deified after her death. The emperor seated on a chair assists in the apotheosis of Sabina, in the presence of the Genius of the Campus Martius. Sabina

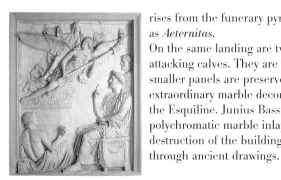

Relief from the Arco di Portogallo:
Hadrian assists in the apotheosis
of Sabina

Panel in *opus sectile*
with polychromatic marbles
from the Basilica of Junius
Bassus, representing a tiger
attacking a calf

rises from the funerary pyre, on the back of a winged female figure identifiable as *Aeternitas*.

On the same landing are two beautiful panels in *opus sectile* representing tigers attacking calves. They are two of the very few surviving elements (another two smaller panels are preserved in the Palazzo Massimo at the Terme) of the extraordinary marble decorations of the so-called "Basilica of Junius Bassus" on the Esquiline. Junius Bassus, consul in 317 AD, built the large hall. Splendid polychromatic marble inlay entirely covered the walls of the large room. After the destruction of the building, the precious wall decorations can be reconstructed only through ancient drawings.

Knight of Arpino,
*Combat of the Horatii
and the Curiatii* (1612-1613),
detail of the fresco in the Hall
of the Horatii and Curiatii

The Conservators' Apartment

The official rooms of the Palazzo dei Conservatori, the so-called "Apartment," have a particular character linked to the function of the areas that received the magistracy of the Conservators, which played a central role in the municipal structure beginning in the middle of the fourteenth century. This magistracy was an expression of a municipal social class formed out of the public nobility that possessed land in the outlying zones of the city and "bovattieri" (merchants) enriched by the commerce in foodstuffs. The magistracy affirmed with pride its autonomy (at least administrative), against the central power tied to the pontifical Curia. The Statutes of the city of Rome, edited in 1363, recognized the power of the Conservators in financial and economic matters. In fact, presiding over the *Camera Urbis*, the Conservators administered and controlled customs and public taxes. The Statutes also recognized the Conservators as a power of control over the Senator who resided in the Palazzo Senatorio. In addition, these Statutes conferred on them the power to nominate other magistrates and offices within the municipal structure. They were able to nominate the leaders and the *magistri viarum*, who were entrusted with important tasks, such as, respectively, the maintenance of public peace and provisions regarding urban activities. The meetings of Public Council and Private Council attest to the central role of the Conservators. The representatives of the municipal social class and Capitoline magistracies participated in these assemblies, conducted in the rooms of the Palazzo dei Conservatori.

Knight of Arpino, *Discovery of the She-wolf* (1595-1596), detail of the fresco in the Hall of the Horatii and Curiatii

Nevertheless, the history and the importance of the role of the Roman Municipality is fully understood only in light of its relationship with the pontifical Curia, of which the Governor of Rome was a member. This office, created under the pontificate of Eugenius IV as direct issuing of papal power, ended up depriving the Capitoline magistracy of its power. In subsequent years, the Conservators lost their effective power and, although continuing to exist, played a purely formal role for many centuries.

Nevertheless, beginning from the last decades of the fifteenth century, with Sixtus IV's donation of bronzes in 1471, and the commission of the first important cycle of frescoes in the official rooms in the first decade of the sixteenth century, the Palazzo dei Conservatori underwent a decorative and artistic renewal, culminating in Michelangelo's projects.

The halls of the Conservators' Apartment testify to the appeal to the ancient greatness of Rome, whose memory is exalted by the representation of examples of civil virtue. They contain important fresco cycles and are elaborately embellished with fine decorative elements, from engraved ceilings to sculpted or decorated doors, from stuccoes of the Chapel to eighteenth century tapestries of the Hall of the Throne, and to priceless ancient bronze statues which they contain. The commissioning of the oldest fresco cycle in the halls of the Apartment took place in the first decade of the sixteenth century. The commission chose for the theme of the cycle stories concerning the birth of the city and *exempla* of courage and virtue in the history of the Roman Republic. The frescoes in the Hall of Hannibal and the Hall of the She-wolf represent the only surviving elements of this cycle. The choice of subjects remained unchanged, even when the rooms assumed a new decorative cycle completed many years later in a definitely different historical and cultural context. The retention of the same theme confers a unitary character to the decoration of the halls of the Apartment and testifies to the endurance of the symbolic significance of the narrative elements through time.

Knight of Arpino,
*Combat of the Horatii
and the Curiatii* (1612-1613),
detail

Hall of the Horatii and Curiatii

The Public Council adjourned in the large hall, which assumed its current
dimensions following Michelangelo's restructuring of the palace. Still today, it is
the site of important ceremonies. For example, it was here that the Treaty of Rome
was signed in 1956, the first and founding act of the European Union.
In 1595, the painter Giuseppe Cesari, known as the Knight of Arpino, was
commissioned to create a new cycle of frescoes in substitution of the preceding one,
for the most part lost. Cesari, who worked with the help of his workshop, conceived
the cycle as tapestries hung along the walls. On the short ends a heavy red curtain,
held up by Telamones, fell onto the scenes. On the long sides, vertical bands
decorated with beautiful garlands of fruits and flowers, trophies of arms, and lustral
vases divide diverse episodes. At the base extends a frieze in imitation marble with
monochrome medallions depicting episodes of Roman history related to the theme
in the fresco located above. The Knight of Arpino referred to the stories of the birth
of Rome and the first kings narrated by the historian Titus Livy in his *Ab urbe
condita libri*. In different periods, the painter created the episodes of the *Discovery
of the She-wolf* (1595-1596), the *Battle against the inhabitants of Veii and Fidenae*
(1598-1601), and the *Combat of the Horatii and the Curiatii* (1612-1613). There

Knight of Arpino,
Rape of the Sabine Women
(1636-1640)

was a long interruption after the completion of these first frescoes. They were not worked on again until 1636, and were completed in 1640, with the creation of the last three episodes: *Rape of the Sabine Women, Numa Pompilius institutes the cult of the Vestals*, and *Romulus sows the furrow of "Roma quadrata."*

Beginning in the second decade of the sixteenth century, statues of the popes were placed in the room as clear recognition of papal authority. Some of these statues were removed for various historical vicissitudes; only two magnificent sculptures remain. One is a statue of Urban VIII Barberini (1623-1644), created by Gian Lorenzo Bernini and his assistants between 1635 and 1640, and another, in bronze in honor of Innocent X Pamphilj (1644-1655), created by Alessandro Algardi between 1646 and 1650. In 1643, the last year of Pope Urban VIII's papacy, the hall was completed with the addition of three inlaid walnut doors, with coats of arms and large quadrangular panels depicting allegorical scenes and legendary episodes of the foundation of Rome and the early kingdom, attributed to the sculptors and engravers Giovan Battista Olivieri and Giovanni Maria Giorgetti.

The statue in honor of Pope Urban VIII, made by Bernini between 1635 and 1640 with assistants, was devised by effecting significant changes to the model of the grandiose bronze statue of the pope realized between 1628 and 1631 for the funereal monument in Saint Peter's Basilica in the Vatican.
If the flowing drapery of the cope and lace-lined vest hark back to the bronze statue in the Vatican, the scope of the arms and hands as well as the slight tilt to the head soften the peremptoriness of the gesture and give the marble effigy an aura of slightly more cordial urbanity. The pope is shown wearing the elaborate vestments used for official occasions: he is wearing the triple-crowned papal tiara, with its three rings of ornaments and jewels. The infulae descend along his sides and they are decorated with the heraldic symbols of the Barberini family. The cope, under which can be glimpsed the minute folds of the vest lined with fretwork lace, is edged with elaborate embroidery and held in place by a polished clasp set with precious stones.

Alessandro Algardi
(Bologna 1598 - Rome 1654)

*Statue in honor of Pope
Innocent X Pamphilj*
In 1645, the Conservators decided
to erect an honorary bronze statue
to the pope. The statue was to be
placed in the Palazzo Nuovo, a
building that Pope Innocent X had
built in the piazza of the Capitoline
Hill. In 1646 the Bolognese
sculptor Alessandro Algardi was
commissioned to make the
statue. The first casting was
flawed, while the second was
acceptable to the commissioners.
The honorary statue, even though
not perfectly smoothed,
considering the urgency with
which it had to be placed in the
piazza of the Capitoline Hill for the
Holy Year celebrations, was
inaugurated in the grand hall of
the Palazzo dei Conservatori on
March 9, 1650. Moved the the
great hall in the Palazzo Nuovo in
1671, the statue was removed
during the late eighteenth-century
French occupation and definitively
placed in the Hall of the Horatii
and Curiatii in 1818. The bronze
statue is by no means perfect,
mainly because of the
imperfections in the casting and
the fact that the surface was not
polished after the casting. This,
however, rather than being a
defect, has given the sculpture its
astonishing force. Even though the
artist did not quite plan it that way,
the "unfinished" effect actually
exalts the work's extraordinary
quality, and many critics consider
it one of Algardi's greatest works.

Wooden door, Hall of the Horatii and Curiatii, 1643
Above, you can see the coat of arms of the Roman people and the magistrates from the first quarter of 1643: the curators Marco Antonio Citarella, Gino Angelo Capponi, Camillo Pamphilj and the prior of the Caporioni Carlo Eustachi. The date, ANO DO. / MDCXXXXIII, can be read in the two scrolls below.
On the left door, in the first panel above, there is an *Allegory of Rome and the Tiber*; below, another panel depicts *Romulus and Remus crowning the She-wolf and milking her*. On the right door, above, we have *Curtius throwing himself into the chasm*; below, *Romulus and Remus crowning the She-wolf and adorning her with wreaths*.

Hall of the Captains

Between 1587 and 1594, painter Tommaso Laureti executed the decoration of the fresco in the room. The fresco depicts the representation and exaltation of the *exempla* of virtue and courage in the episodes of *Mucius Scaevola and Porsenna*, *Horatius Cocles on the Pons Sublicius*, the *Justice of Brutus*, and the *Victory at Lake Regillus*, following the narration of the Roman historian Titus Livy. The Sicilian painter, summoned to Rome by Gregory XIII to paint the ceiling of the Hall of Constantine, narrated the historical episodes with monumental flare and lively colors. His pictorial language is full of references to the paintings of Michelangelo. This is very clear in the details of the fresco of *Mucius Scaevola and Porsenna*. In addition, there is no doubt that the *Justice of Brutus* recalls the works of Raphael. This fresco, because it is located in the room where the Conservators sat in the tribunal, acquires a particular symbolic value.

Beginning in the last decade of the sixteenth century, this room, second for its dimensions and the richness of the decorations only to the Hall of the Horatii and Curiatii, was designated to celebrate, alongside the virtue of the ancient ancestors, the wisdom of famous men and the valor of leaders of the Pontifical State. Thus, funerary inscriptions were inserted in the walls. Among them, the most noteworthy is the portrait created in memory of Virginio Cesarini (1624), by either Bernini or Duquesnoy (opinions vary). This is considered unanimously the most significant work of Roman sculpture in the first decades of the seventeenth century. In addition, many statues in honor of the Captains were located in the hall. To create these statues, ancient material was frequently reused and reworked. For example, reuse is visible in the statue in honor of Alessandro Farnese (in 1593, with the portrait by sculptor Ippolito Buzi) and the colossal statue celebrating Marcantonio Colonna who, at the command of the pontifical fleet, contributed to the victory of the Christian armada in the battle of Lepanto in 1571. In 1630, in order to honor Carlo Barberini, brother of Urban VIII, the sculptor Alessandro Algardi was entrusted with the restoration of a torso of a Roman cuirassed statue. He completed the statue by adding legs and arms, in addition to a prestigious shield. Bernini sculpted the portrait of the general with great efficacy.

Finally, there are two sculptures depicting Gianfrancesco Aldobrandini and Tommaso Rospigliosi, by Ercole Ferrata.

Tommaso Laureti,
Justice of Brutus
(1587-1594)

Tommaso Laureti,
Victory at Lake Regillus
(1587-1594)

Hall of the Triumphs

In 1569, when the external façade of the palace was still under construction, painters Michele Alberti and Iacopo Rocchetti (or Rocca), pupils of Daniele da Volterra, were commissioned to paint a frieze in fresco extending along the length of the walls. The room derives its current name from this frieze. It depicts the triumph of the consul Lucius Aemilius Paullus over Perseus, king of Macedonia, celebrated in 167 BC. The ancient historian Plutarch records the episode with great detail. The painters narrated with vivacity and richness the development of the conqueror's procession over the course of three days, echoing the model of historical classical reliefs. The representation of the consul's ascent to the Capitoline Hill (according to the ancient custom) appears on the external wall that faces the city. However, the renewed façade of the Palazzo dei Conservatori substitutes the Temple of Capitoline Jupiter, as the final point of the triumphal procession, in an playful allusion recalling past and present.

Shortly before (1568), the carpenter Flaminio Bolonger completed the wooden ceiling of the room. By recuperating the chromatic richness of the wooden ceiling coffers, recent restorations restituted importance to the prestigious engravings of the frames and of the beams and the finely modeled trophies of arms located in the coffers.

Two paintings were commissioned for this room: the *Deposition*, by Paolo Piazza in 1614 and *Saint Francesca Romana* by Giovanni Francesco Romanelli. In 1638, the Conservators commissioned the latter work in honor of the patron saint of the city. Pietro da Cortona executed another large painting in the room: the *Battle of Alexander versus Darius*. According to the most recent study, the painting was completed in the fifth decade of the seventeenth century in order to celebrate Alessandro Sacchetti, commander of the pope's troops. In this painting, the Tuscan painter demonstrates complete mastery of his art, expressed with great skill and fluency.

Added to the Capitoline Hill through Sixtus IV's donation, this beautiful bronze statue is characterized by eyes in silver inlay. It was interpreted for many years as a Gypsy because of its soft and elegant hairstyle, feminine facial features, and dress softly draped over the body. The shape of the dress and comparison of this work with other statues suggest, instead, that this is a classical work of the first century AD. It depicts a youth responsible for a cult (*camillus*). The right hand once held a small cup used for ritual libations.

The small bronze statue, depicting a boy in the act of pulling a thorn out of his foot, was added to the Capitoline Hill in 1471, as part of Sixtus IV's donation of the Lateran bronzes to the People of Rome. The singular and particularly graceful pose of the figure, portrayed in an unusual position, made this work one of the most appreciated and copied during the Renaissance. At the same time, the unique pose of the statue created numerous questions regarding its identity. It is an eclectic work, probably conceived in the first century BC, formed from Hellenistic models of the third-second century BC for the body, with a head derived from Greek works of the fifth century BC.

Capitoline Brutus

In 1564, Cardinal Pius da Carpi donated to the museum the magnificent bronze portrait of extraordinary expressive force. The identification of the statue with Junius Brutus, the first Roman consul, represents an astute interpretation of the antiquarian culture.
However, this assertion is without any real foundation. Although the statue possesses features referable to Greek portrait models of poets and philosophers, a problematic understanding of the work of art suggests that it is the product of a powerful reinterpretation of the Roman artistic culture of the Republican age. Therefore, the statue dates between the fourth and third centuries BC. The extreme rarity of bronze portraits in this period, together with the possibility of such an ancient date, renders this work one of the most precious in the Capitoline collections.

Detail of the coffered ceiling

Hall of the She-wolf

Until the seventeenth century, the room was a loggia with three arches facing the city. It was decorated with frescoes belonging to the first pictorial embellishment of the Apartment of the Conservators. In the sixteenth century, the presence of the She-wolf, among other sculptures, was documented in this space. During research conducted in 1957, traces of the arches were marked on the external wall. These constitute the only visible remains of the loggia preserved today.
The frescoes are generally dated to the years 1508-1513. The insertion of the Consular *Fasti*, first, and then the inscriptions honoring Alessandro Farnese and Marcantonio Colonna (whose military exploits were celebrated next to the Capitoline *Fasti*), irreversibly damaged the frescoes. It is difficult to understand the frescoes because of their fragmentary condition. The scene of triumph is identified as the *Triumph of Lucius Aemilius Paullus*, and battle episode is identified as the *Campaign against the Tolostobogians*.
Following restoration of the entire room in 1865, a wooden coffered ceiling was installed. It is still visible today. Recent restoration revived the decorative vivacity of the ceiling. The background of the coffers contains pleasant, quickly executed anthropomorphic forms interweaving with floral decorations, an obvious referral to sixteenth century *grotesques*.

They were discovered in the Roman Forum in the sixteenth century. The precious inscriptions originally decorated the Parthian Arch of Augustus, dedicated in 19 BC. The inscriptions, which represent irreplaceable documents for the understanding of Roman history, contain lists of the consuls from 483-19 BC and lists of triumphators from 753-19 BC. A precious fragment records the name of Romulus, founder of the city. Immediately after their discovery, Michelangelo used the Capitoline *Fasti* as wall decorations on the back wall of the palace courtyard. In 1586, the *Fasti* were moved to their current location, with a systematization that recalls their arrangement in the courtyard.

The statue is located in the center of the room, where in the sixteenth century Aldrovandi recalls that it was, "in a covered loggia that overlooks the urban plain." (The traces of the columns of the loggia are visible on the wall between the two windows.)
The She-wolf, with its extraordinary evocative power, is the symbol of the city. The donation of Sixtus IV brought the statue to the Capitoline Hill. Initially, it stood in the fifteenth century façade of the palace. Then, it was transferred inside the palace, on the occasion of Michelangelo's architectural interventions. At that time, the twins were added, attributed to some by Pollaiolo. They transformed the ancient Lateran symbol of justice into *"Mater Romanorum."*
The creation of the work, which in origin probably had nothing to do with the legend of the origins of Rome, is attributable to a fifth century BC workshop in Etruria or Magna Graecia.

Bust of
Michelangelo Buonarroti

Hall of the Geese

The room is named after the small bronze works that Pope Benedict XIII purchased from the Chartusians of Santa Maria degli Angeli and donated to the Conservators in 1727. Placed in a precious architectural stucco cornice with the donator's name, the group of works was evidently connected to the legend that said the Capitoline Hill had been saved from the Gallic invasion in 390 BC by a group of geese that sounded the alarm. The central piece is of particular interest, a bronze vase in the shape of the bust of Isis, depicting the jewels that decorate the figure of the deity of Egyptian origins in great detail.

Recent restorations recuperated the pleasing decorative unity of the room by freeing the sixteenth century ceiling from the cumbersome additions and secondary paintings. In this way, the coffered ceiling acquired its original "sky blue" color on the background where gilded decorations of fine workmanship (rosettes of various forms, lustral vases, shields) are located. The rediscovered colors harmonize well with the vivacious colors of the frieze where elegant decorative elements alternating with trophies of flowers, fruits, and weapons frame scenes depicting ancient games on the background of real and fantastic landscapes. Among these is a view of the piazza of the Capitoline Hill before Paul III Farnese's interventions (1534-1549) with a faithful reproduction of the Church of the Aracoeli. Due to a lack of documents, the fresco is associated with Paul III because of the lily of justice visible on the shield. The work is attributed to various artists. According to the most recent hypothesis, the artist belonged to the circle of Flemish artists active in Rome in the third and fourth decades of the sixteenth century.

In the eighteenth century, the room was enriched by decorations of gilt stucco to frame some works donated to the Capitoline and other works already located in the room, for example, a copy of Francesco Penni's painting *The Holy Family*. The statue of Medusa, placed on an ancient base, has been located in this room since its donation to the Capitoline (1731). Notwithstanding different dates, scholars have recognized unanimously that it is a work of Bernini. Similarly, in the eighteenth century, a bronze portrait of Michelangelo on a bust of *bigio* marble was donated to the Capitoline.

*Bust of the Medusa
(1630s-1640s)*
According to Ovid, the mythical Medusa had the power to turn to stone anyone who looked directly at her.
Bernini's is a veritable portrait of the most beautiful and deadly of the Gorgons (this is, in fact, a Bust, and not a truncated Head) at the very moment of her metamorphosis. The classical myth is re-evoked according to the contents of a poem by Giovan Battista Marino ("I do not know if mortal chisel sculpted me thus, / or, in reflecting myself in a clear glass, / sight of myself made me such", from *La Galeria*, 1630, I, 272): Medusa, looking into an imaginary mirror and seeing her own reflection, is represented just as she realises, with horror and anguish, the mockery of it all. Right before our eyes she is being transformed into marble.
Bernini intended his Medusa to be a refined Baroque metaphor for sculpture and the virtue of the sculptor, who has the power to "petrify" those who admire his extraordinary ability to use a chisel.

Table

The room contains two glass display cases housing a rich collection of ancient marbles. In the center of the room is a precious table decorated along the border with scenes from the life of Achilles. The work, which originally had a cult function, depicts in a continuous narrative cycle some of the most significant episodes from the life of the Greek hero, very popular in the fourth century BC. The original element was reutilized in the cosmatesque decoration from the Church of the Aracoeli. This decoration is a prestigious work of colored marble inlay that exalts the ingenuous but efficient figural ornamentation.

View of the Colosseum
(circa 1544)

Hall of the Eagles

The decoration of this small, refined room is contemporaneous with the decoration of the preceding room. In the Hall of the Eagles, a frieze painted with prestigious *grotesques* extends under the rich wooden ceiling where painted scenes alternate with depressions decorated with gilded and engraved rosettes. Among the scenes depicted in the frieze, the image of the piazza on the Capitoline Hill is an interesting document. It depicts the newly arrived equestrian statue of Marcus Aurelius and the start of interventions regarding the transformation of the palaces.

Wooden ceiling
(1544)

Tapestry with the goddess Roma

Hall of the Tapestries

The room owes its current appearance to eighteenth century interventions. In 1770, the room was renewed entirely to host the canopy (baldacchino) of the papal throne. Precious tapestries commissioned to the Roman factory of San Michele adorned the walls. Thereafter, the doors were finely decorated and gilded. The doorframes were made in colored marble (*diaspro* from Sicily). The painter Domenico Corvi created the models for the tapestries. The subjects of the tapestries reproduced works housed on the Capitoline Hill, e.g., Pieter Paul Rubens' painting of the *Romulus and Remus suckled by the She-wolf* (which became part of the Capitoline Picture Gallery) and the sculpture of the goddess Roma, the so-called "Cesi Roma" (preserved in the courtyard of the Palazzo dei Conservatori). The other two subjects also depict images that exalt the civic virtues of the ancient ancestors: the *Vestal Tuccia* and the *Master of Faleri*. Since 1544, according to the date recorded in a cartouche, the frescoed frieze, depicting the life of Scipio Africanus, alternates with painted images of ancient sculptures in the room. Traditionally, the fresco is attributed to Daniele da Volterra, but more probably an artist from his circle created the work. In the same years, a rich ceiling with hexagonal coffers with a blue background was executed. The ceiling contains gilded engravings with helmets, shields, and parade arms. The refurbished painted surface of the blue background enhances the recent restoration of the precious gilding. The consoles and the engraved and gilded wooden table, also dating to the eighteenth century, contribute to the richness of the room.

Workshop of Iacopo Ripanda,
Hannibal in Italy
(circa 1508-1509)

Hall of Hannibal

The Hall of Hannibal is the only room that entirely preserves the original decoration of the frescoes from the Apartment dating to the first decade of the sixteenth century. Recent studies have cast doubt on the traditional attribution to the Bolognese painter Iacopo Ripanda. Although recognizing his presence on the Capitoline, indeed attested to by the literary sources, studies have not clarified whether the artist was the principal figure involved in the production of the fresco or a collaborator. The frescoes refer to the episodes of the Punic War and are framed by pilasters adorned with candelabra on a gold background. Under the scenes extends a frieze that was repainted many times. It depicts niches containing painted busts of Roman generals.

The episodes, narrated with antiquarian taste, refer to the *Triumph of Rome over Sicily*, *Hannibal in Italy*, *Peace negotiations between Lutatius Catulus and Hamilcar*, and the *Naval Battle*, traditionally identified as the battle of the Aegatians. Executed between 1516 and 1519, this wooden ceiling is the oldest ceiling in the palace. The seventeenth century inventories of the Apartment already documented noteworthy damage to the ceiling. Restoration has recuperated the elegant blue color of the background, reinvigorated by beautiful, gilded engravings. In particular, the representation of the twins with the She-wolf is very noticeable, given its position in the center of the cross vault.

This splendidly decorated bronze vase placed in the center of the room evokes the sumptuous triumphal processions that took place in conclusion of wars of conquest in the East. During the procession, the most precious works of art taken from the enemy were put on display. In fact, an inscription engraved on the edge records the name of Mithridates VI, king of Pontus (163-120 BC). The vase arrived in Italy as Sulla or Pompey's spoil of war. The vase was found in Antium, in the Villa of Nero.

Benedict XIV donated it to the museum in the eighteenth century.

The Chapel

After 1870, the Chapel of the palace was changed with the deconstruction of the altar and the creation of a new door. Restructuring the Capitoline complex, with the creation of new museum itineraries, allowed the reorganization of the old Chapel. Now the environment is recomposed through the reinstallation of the altar on the back wall. The altar is decorated with a rich frontal embellished with precious colored marble inlay. Adorned with the bees of the Barberini crest, the altar was executed under the pontificate of Urban VIII (1623-1644). The original altar-piece, a slate that Marcello Venusti painted for the Capitoline in 1577-1578, depicts *Mary between Saints Peter and Paul before the background of Rome*. Between 1575-1578 Michele Alberti and Iacopo Rocchetti, already active on the Capitoline, completed the fresco and stucco decorations of the Chapel. The Chapel is dedicated to Mary and the protective saints of the city, Peter and Paul. The frescoes inserted in the vaults illustrate the episodes from the lives of the two saints. The canvas paintings of the Evangelists and Roman saints attributed to Giovanni Francesco Romanelli (1645-1648) complete the rich decoration of the Chapel. Finally, the fresco of the *Madonna with Child and Angels* is by Andrea d'Assisi. Torn out from its original location in the ancient loggia of the palace, it was transferred to the landing of the staircase. In the nineteenth century, it was moved to cover the grate that allowed the Conservators and their entourage to assist in the religious ceremonies from the Hall of the Captains.

Crater of Aristonothos,
detail

The Castellani Halls

Situated at the end of the museum itinerary that winds its way through the interior of the
Apartment of the Conservators, the Castellani Halls house a valuable range of materials
that represent the actual formation of the historic collections of the museum. Indeed, the
extraordinary heritage of the Capitoline Museums boasts two considerable collections
of archaeological material, both of which were amassed in the second half of the
nineteenth century: the Castellani Collection and the Collection of the Artistic Industrial
Museum.

The Castellani Collection in the Capitoline Museums
The objects exhibited in these two rooms were donated to the Capitoline Museums by
Augusto Castellani, a famous goldsmith and collector who lived in Rome in the second
half of the nineteenth century. He played a key role in the administrative and cultural life
of the city holding, amongst other positions, that of director of the Capitoline Museums.
He enriched the museum collections with his first considerable donation in 1867,
which was then followed by a second one in 1876, which was just as large.

The first donation in 1867 is remembered in a deliberation in which the Roman Magistracy thanked Augusto Castellani for having given the Municipality "a collection of Tyrrhenian vases" and issued a decree to coin a medal that is now housed in the Capitoline Medal Collection. The second, in 1876, was a vast collection of antique objects which he donated to the museum over a span of more than a decade: as we can see from the Council proposal, he intended to bequeath everything under the sole condition that it was to remain the property of the Municipality for ever.

The Collection of the Artistic Industrial Museum
The museum, initially founded as the Museum of Applied Industrial Arts, was conceived by several key figures on the nineteenth-century Roman cultural scene, such as Prince Baldassarre Odescalchi, Augusto Castellani and his brother Alessandro, inviting the Municipality of Rome to "take the initiative to found a permanent exhibition of objects of industrial applied arts in our city," based on the model of those created in Paris and London. The archaeological collection housed in the Capitoline Museums represents a limited part of the vast collections of the Artistic Industrial Museum, the various contents of which were destined to diverse Roman museum institutions in the 1950s. Of all the members of the Board of Directors of the Museum of Applied Industrial Arts (Artistic Industrial Museum), Augusto and Alessandro Castellani were the most active in collecting extremely valuable material that they then donated to the museum.

Attic red-figure *kylix*. Pentathlete depicted from behind.
In the style of the Onesimos Painter, first three decades, fifth century BC

Attic red-figure *kylix*. Athlete drawing water from a well. In the style of the Onesimos Painter, first three decades, fifth century BC

Castellani Hall I

The Castellani Collection includes around 700 finds from the most important archaeological sites from Etruria, Latium and Magna Graecia, covering a chronological time span that goes from the eighth to the fourth century BC. Using criteria that were common in the nineteenth century, Castellani divided the finds according to class, without taking into consideration any possible associations between the groups of objects amassed together. He also included no detailed description of the origin of the materials, although it was sometimes possible to reconstruct this using the documentation available. The necropolis of the main Etruscan cities (Veii, Cerveteri, Tarquinia and Vulci) were his favourite destinations, with the addition of other sites in Latium such as Palestrina, the centers of Sabina, the Falisco countryside (Civita Castellana) and obviously Rome. Furthermore, Alessandro Castellani, who lived in Naples for many years, also gave his brother a lot of material from sites in Campania and Southern Italy. While reproposing the division established by Castellani, in the current exhibition emphasis is placed on the pottery, both that imported from Greece (Hall I) and that produced locally (Hall II). The quantity, but even more so the quality of the material on show makes it possible to follow the development of Greek production from the eighth to the fourth century BC, with samples that are of considerable importance and excellently preserved. From the second half of the eighth century BC until the middle of the sixth century BC the pottery produced in Corinth was present throughout the Mediterranean and it must have been part of the luxury goods produced for the classes that were better off both financially and socially. Belonging to the same period was also the Greek-Oriental pottery produced along the coast of Asia Minor and the nearby Greek islands such as Samos, Rhodes and Chios, which were mainly exported to Magna Graecia, Sicily and Etruria, where the trade and artistic contacts with the Greek-Oriental world had important consequences that conditioned the development of handicraft and artistic production. However, the best represented pottery category is the one produced in Athens from the beginning of the sixth to the fourth century BC, characterized by reddish colored clay with rich decorative illustrations: depending on the technique used, the production is either in red-figure and black-figure pottery. The Attic vases, most of which come from the necropolis in Etruria, are one of the soundest tools for the construction of the history and artisan and artistic production of not only Greek civilization, but also of the others that were active in the Mediterranean basin. In particular, in Etruria such an extensive presence of these "merchandise vases" – in the middle of the sixth century AD a city such as Vulci absorbed a higher quantity of Attic products than the largest Greek cities – makes them a main vehicle for the transmission of Hellenic iconography and therefore also of the knowledge linked to them, such as the myth and *epos*, which played a key role in determining the process of acculturization of the dominant elites and those who commissioned and purchased these goods. As well as the Attic vases on show in these halls, there are also ones with red figures but of Apulian and Lucan production, created in the workshops of Magna Graecia between the end of the fifth and fourth century AD.

Crater of Aristonothos

This is a masterpiece of Archaic pottery decoration. According to the "Bullettino di Corrispondenza Archeologica" of 1869, this was bought at the time by Augusto Castellani, in Cerveteri; the pottery was then included in the second donation, in 1876, as can be seen in the old museum inventories, where it is noted as a "reddish clay vase with figures in dark color. On one side there are five warriors attacking a sixth warrior who has fallen to the ground. On the other there is a naval battle with two ships, the first of which with three warriors and sundry

sailors, the second with only three warriors." The crater is richly decorated with two extremely complex scenes. On one side there is the well-known episode, narrated in the *Odyssey*, of Polyphemus' blinding: Odysseus' four friends are shown being helped by Odysseus himself (the first on the right) as they thrust a stake into the Cyclop's eye. Odysseus is depicted with his leg against a wall of the cavern to push himself forward with greater force. On the other side there is a naval battle: on the left there is a flat-hulled warship with rowers, on which

there are four warriors with helmet, spear and shield, one of whom is standing aft at the helm; on the right there is a merchant ship, with a deeper, curved hull and sail; here there are also four armed men, one of whom, the sentry, is in the crows-nest. Regardless of the fact that the naval battle has been given different interpretations, what is clear is that this is a skirmish between Etruscans and Greeks. The latter, who had settled in colonies in Sicily and Campania, were soon clashing with the thalassocrat Etruscans, who dominated the Tyrrhenian.

This large crater, set on a trumpet-shaped pedestal, was used at aristocratic feasts for pouring wine. Besides the complex painted decorations, it is also signed by the Greek potter who made it: "*Aristonothos epoiesen.*" Aristonothos was obviously an artisan who, after leaving Greece, arrived in opulent Etruria in about the second quarter of the seventh century BC, where he settled in Cerveteri. It was here that a member of the aristocratic class presumably commissioned the crater for his sumptuous feasts.

In one of the showcases in the hall there is a remarkable terracotta artefact depicting a seated male figure, listed in the earliest of the museum's manuscript inventories as a "small seated terracotta statue representing a character with his right hand poised as if in thought." This is one of the three small statues recovered in 1865 in the Tomb of the Five Chairs in Cerveteri. They were then bought by Augusto Castellani along with several gold jewels, and the following year Castellani included the male figure in his first donation of objects to the Capitoline Museums, while the other two were sold to the British Museum. There were originally five statues, but two were lost due to their parlous state. These two were figures seated on chairs sculpted from tufa and placed in a room off the lobby (reconstruction by Prayon, 1974). The fact that there was also an altar in the same room and that the figures were shown with their hand outstretched as if asking for or receiving an offering makes it probable that the rooms was a small domestic sacellum dedicated to the family's forebears. In Etruria, in fact, there was a deeply-felt devotion to ancestors, as can be evinced from the statues of forebears lining the long entrance corridors and vestibules to tombs and used in evoking ancestors in ritual ceremonies.

The figure represented in the small statue is opulently dressed in a large red cape, an obvious sign of high bearing, which is clasped at the shoulder by a carefully crafted oriental-like fibula. The Greek writer Dionysius of Halicarnassus, in fact, mentions that one of the trappings of supreme power used by Etruscan kings was a "dark red tunic with gold decorations and an embroidered crimson mantle." These symbols of status and power were then passed on to the Roman world. Chronologically, the work can be dated to the second half of the seventh century BC, when Cerveteri was an important center for the production of noteworthy coroplastic production. In fact, the art of modelling clay was "the national art of the Etruscans," and their masterpieces, such as the Veii Apollo and the Sarcophagus "degli Sposi," were and are familiar to all.

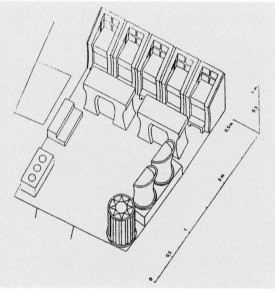

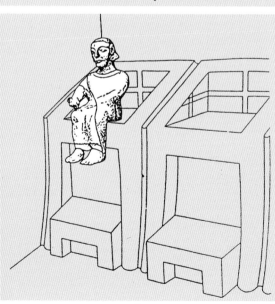

Bas-reliefs from the Tomb of the Dogs, Tolfa

The three artefacts, "no. 3 four-holed artefacts worked in the Archaic manner with representations of animals," were deposited by Augusto Castellani in the Capitoline Museums in 1872 and were part of his second donation of 1876. The 1866 "Bullettino di Corrispondenza Archeologica" states that the grey tufa bas-reliefs, along with a large number of other objects, were originally taken from a tomb vault, known as the Tomb of the Dogs, located in Tolfa in the Pian della Conserva. As was often the case in that period, nobody bothered to note the relationships between the diverse objects that were then sold to different museums; the reliefs, bought by Augusto Castellani, simply arrived as they were at the Capitoline Museums.

Recent analysis has revealed the interior of the tomb and its decorations (reconstruction by Naso, 1993): the bas-reliefs, sculpted along the main sides of the sepulchral couches along the three sides of the room, depicted a dog (in the two side panels) and a stag (central panel). They were unfortunately damaged and reduced to fragments during removal, and were then reassembled despite the many missing sections. However, it can be stated that the relief was of a hunting scene including two dogs, one of which sniffing the ground, that converged towards the center as they hunted the stag. Considering the richness of the decorations, this is almost certainly the burial site of a member of the aristocratic class, for whom hunting was a distinctive pastime.

In the Archaic period, in fact, the upper echelons of society built large family tombs, almost entirely dug out of tufa rock, with a large main room along whose walls were set out the sepulchral couches and elaborate decorations.

The fact that this context has been dated to the first half of the sixth century BC is perfectly in keeping with the chronology of Etruscan-Corynthian ceramics, from which the animal figures have been drawn.

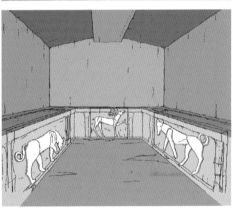

Castellani Hall II

Continuing with the division established by Castellani, this hall also houses the pottery produced locally in the Etruscan-Latian domain. Unfortunately, even more so than was the case for the Greek pottery, Castellani omitted to mention their precise origins or any possible associations, and it is only thanks to recent studies carried out on these categories of materials that it is possible to identify some of the production centers with certain accuracy.

The pottery of impasto and bucaro exhibited in this hall are two productions that were typical of the Etruscan-Latian area and that were partially contemporary and correlated (seventh-sixth century AD).

Impasto pottery is understood here as pottery produced with a mixture of clay and microscopic fragments of minerals, present in varying concentrations. At first production was manual but in the period in question it was then replaced by the lathe, which made the sides of the objects even thinner and the firing more homogeneous. The main types of impasto found in this area are those of brown impasto, fine brown impasto and red impasto; the surface was polished and brightened and embellished with various decorative techniques that included engraving, excision, stamping and painting; in some cases there was also plastic decoration with small figures or animals heads on the tops of handles, the edges or as lid handles.

Most of the impasto pottery production was crockery for the dining-table, the kitchen or storage, such as the *pithoi* that were used to preserve foodstuffs; objects for the household were also created in impasto, such as the large brackets to support the vases or the braziers to warm the rooms.

Bucaro was also an impasto pottery but it was much more refined than its predecessors: the clay was purified, additions minute and production was done only with the lathe. Its black, homogeneous color was probably due to perfect firing in surroundings rich in iron oxide. Initially extremely thin, the sides gradually became heavier over the decades; the shining surfaces were decorated both with engravings and in relief and with plastic additions. As regards the shapes, most of them copied those of the impasto production such as the *kantharos*, the chalice or the pail, while a quantitatively smaller group copied those of the pottery imported from Greece, as was the case with the *skyphos*, the *kotyle* and the *olpe*. Furthermore, in some cases it is also possible to hypothesise a derivation from objects made of precious materials, such as ivory or bronze.

In grave trappings, the quantity of bucaro is just a little greater than that in Greek pottery while lower than that of impasto pottery that is evidence that it was considered to be valuable crockery. Furthermore, recent studies have also shown that not just individual pieces of this pottery were left in the graves, but rather in "services," both for dining and toilet.

One last aspect that is of great interest regards the considerable exportation of bucaro from the settlements of central-southern Etruria to markets throughout the

Mediterranean: in the East, around a thousand samples were exported, frequently associated with amphorae that contained wine.

This hall also houses the painted and illustrated pottery of Etruscan production: the name of Etruscan-geometric is understood as a class of painted pottery that originated as the imitation of Greek products that were diffused throughout Etruria during the first half of the eighth century AD. These objects were made of purified clay worked on the lathe and painted with ornamental motives with horizontal stripes, in squares and diamond shapes, or in metope squares enclosing animal figures such as birds and horses.

Another important category of painted pottery produced in Etruria is the so-called Etruscan-Corinthian category, understood as the pottery produced in Etruria in imitation of Corinthian pottery and produced for almost a century, in particular in the centers of southern and coastal Etruria, starting in the last thirty years of the seventh century AD until the last decade of the sixth century AD.

Replacing the Etruscan-Corinthian pottery, the Etruscan black-figure pottery began to be produced in the middle of the sixth century AD when the main objective of Etruscan culture was that of divulging the *epos* and Greek myths that had been brought to Etruria by means of the imported pottery. In the field of black-figure production many workshops and painters have been identified who were active in the main Etruscan centers from the middle of the sixth to the middle of the fifth century AD. Etruscan red-figure pottery began during the fifth century AD as a result of the influence of the Attic red-figure production. Quantitatively this production was considerable, with workshops that created valuable objects but that was soon to undergo extensive standardization.

On show in this hall is also a limited selection of archaeological finds from the collections of the Artistic Industrial Museum. These are valuable finds of Attic production, with black figures, red figures, and a white background as well of Laconian and Apulian production.

Another aspect of nineteenth century collecting in Rome is represented by a single object which is of outstanding importance: the Tragliatella *oinochoe* which was discovered during excavations carried out near the Bracciano Lake in the area of ancient Cerveteri and was donated to the Capitoline Museums in 1964 in memory of Tommaso Tittoni. This is an Etruscan-Corinthian work, belonging to the Group of Polychrome Vases, and datable to the last thirty years of the seventh century AD. The polychrome *oinochoe* is richly decorated with engravings on three registers which has found various explanations: however, it would appear that the story refers to the saga of Theseus and Ariadne and was reinterpreted for the use and consumption of the Etruscan customer. Putting aside the variety of its possible origins, the most important aspect is certainly the arrival of the Greek myth in Etruria and with it, a life style of Greek origins, which was then adopted by the upper class, thus favoring the process of acculturization and Hellenization that the "principes" wanted to set in motion.

Bronze bicone and silver cist from the so-called "Castellani Tomb" of Palestrina

Other particularly valuable objects such as the bronze *tensa* on show in the next hall also belong to the Castellani Collection. The latter, which is included in the list of the second donation (1876) as "Tensa or biga in bronze from Roman territory, location uncertain," was purchased and reduced to minute fragments by Augusto who, with the help of his son Alfredo, undertook a complicated restoration process which resulted in a totally subjective reconstruction of the artefact, and even going so far as to join different pieces together.

The so-called "Castellani Tomb" of Palestrina

The set of objects, bought by Augusto Castellani in the Latium city of Palestrina, in the showcase are better known as the "Castellani Tomb" of Palestrina because they have long been thought of as a distinct collection derived from one single tomb. In truth, Castellani bought the pieces, along with other objects, and then apportioned them, after a series of vicissitudes, among the Capitoline, Villa Giulia and British Museums. In particular, as far as the material at the Capitoline Museums is concerned, all we need to do is take a look at the inventories to see how they did not come to the museum as a discrete unit; nor does Castellani himself ever to refer to a unique set of objects but to a series of artefacts that were "found together."

Another very interesting aspect is that Castellani decided to restore the objects to improve their aesthetic appearance: the restoration actually amounted to a completely arbitrary reworking of the objects that, in some cases, led him to put together fragments from completely different artefacts.

The objects housed at the Capitoline Museums are,

nonetheless, extremely interesting and can mainly be traced back to oriental-like tomb decorations destined for members of the Prenestino aristocracy: the term "oriental-like" describes that phenomenon by which eastern of oriental objects and motifs were imitated and circulated throughout the Italian peninsula as well as in Greece and the Iberian peninsula between the eighth and seventh centuries BC. In this period the emerging members of individual communities, the so-called "principes," reaffirmed the value of their *status* via a series of highly-ideologized rites, and above all through the use of extremely ornamental tomb decorations. These decorations reflect the aristocracy's customs and include personal objects such as bracelets, breast plates, rings and pendants; objects used for banquets such as silverware and bronze-ware; artefacts emphasizing the aristocrats' roles in life (thrones, flabella, fans) or lauding their warring vocation (shields, sceptres and carts). These luxury items were originally imported, but were then produced locally, at first by Eastern and Greek artisans who had moved to Etruria and then by locals who

were allowed into their workshops. The princely tombs found in Etruria include the Regolini-Galassi Tomb in Cerveteri, the Duce and the Littore Tombs in Vetulonia, the Avori Tomb in Marsigliana D'Albenga and the Barberini and Bernardini Tombs in Palestrina, Latium. The objects on display span a rather wide-ranging period of time, from the laminated bronze bicone vase (which Castellani also heavily reworked), comparable to artefacts from the closing third of the eighth century BC, and the bronze patera, with hulled walls, of oriental derivation and quite common in the Italic-Etruscan context from the second half of the eighth century BC.

As part of this set there are also two silver objects which it is presumed were produced locally, in Cerveteri: a patera decorated with rusticated circular rows concentrically placed around the central medallion, dated to the opening decades of the seventh century BC; and a globular chalice, with decorative motifs engraved under the lip, dated to the second quarter of the seventh century BC.

Of the objects exhibited, the most singular is certainly the cist, which Castellani reconstructed in its

entirety. He had the different pieces of embossed, carved or chiselled silver plates glued to a wooden, cylindrical form he himself had made. The end result is an obviously reworked object that recent analyses have revealed to be put together with pieces from different objects.

No less interesting are the *faïence* objects, including three small new year flasks, inaugural objects given as presents on the first day of the year and filled with scented essences, a globular aryballos with diamond decorations, also used as a container for ointments, and a statue-shaped amulet of the god Nefertum. All of these were presumably made in Egypt during the sixth century BC.

Halls of the Modern Fasti

Going back to the large staircase, one comes to the Halls of the *Fasti*. Along the walls are the inscriptions in memory of the names of the civic magistrates who succeeded one another in the leadership of Rome from 1640 on. After the pair of statues of the Velletri Athletes, Roman copies from fourth century AD originals, one can admire a splendid sarcophagus with Dionysian scenes. Here Dionysus is reclining on a cart led by the Centaurs. He is surrounded by all the figures that are part of his world: Ariadne, Pan, Satyrs and Maenads are all taking part in the festive procession, dancing and playing instruments.

The Dionysian themes are some of the most popular in the Roman world because the mysteries linked to the mythology of the gods and inebriation from wine contain subtle but indissoluble ties with the world hereafter. The well-preserved polychromy highlights the meticulous shaping of the figures.

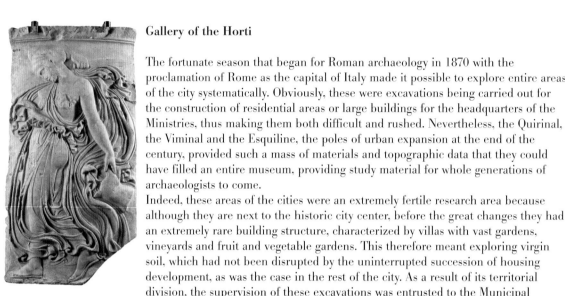

Relief with Maenad,
from a Kallimachos original

Gallery of the Horti

The fortunate season that began for Roman archaeology in 1870 with the proclamation of Rome as the capital of Italy made it possible to explore entire areas of the city systematically. Obviously, these were excavations being carried out for the construction of residential areas or large buildings for the headquarters of the Ministries, thus making them both difficult and rushed. Nevertheless, the Quirinal, the Viminal and the Esquiline, the poles of urban expansion at the end of the century, provided such a mass of materials and topographic data that they could have filled an entire museum, providing study material for whole generations of archaeologists to come.

Indeed, these areas of the cities were an extremely fertile research area because although they are next to the historic city center, before the great changes they had an extremely rare building structure, characterized by villas with vast gardens, vineyards and fruit and vegetable gardens. This therefore meant exploring virgin soil, which had not been disrupted by the uninterrupted succession of housing development, as was the case in the rest of the city. As a result of its territorial division, the supervision of these excavations was entrusted to the Municipal Archaeological Commission: for this reason the extraordinary documentation on an urban phenomenon, on the borders of the public and private sphere and chronologically between the end of the Republic and the beginning of the Imperial age could be added to the Capitoline archaeological collections. The issue in question are the *horti*, i.e. residential complexes immerged in green and characterized by their spectacular decorative structure, born on the edges of the monumental center as the prestigious homes of the most famous noble families of the late Republic and which later became the property of the Empire. In the first Imperial age, the *horti* created an uninterrupted crown of green around the city center, not unlike the villas of nobility in modern Rome: the very situation that the building works at the end of the nineteenth century were gradually endangering. Chronicles from that period give the actual numbers of the discoveries made during those works: "705 amphorae with noteworthy inscriptions; 2,360 terracotta lanterns; 1,824 inscriptions engraved in marble or stone; 77 columns of rare marble; 313 column pieces; 157 marble capitals; 118 plinths; 590 works of art made of terracotta; 405 works of art in bronze; 711 gems, engraved stones and cameos; 18 marble sarcophagi; 152 bas-reliefs; 192 marble statues in good condition; 21 animal figures in marble; 266 busts and heads; 54 pictures in polychrome mosaic; 47 gold objects and 39 silver objects; 36,679 coins of gold, silver and bronze; and an incredible amount of small terracotta relics, or rather, bone, glass, enamel, lead, ivory, bronze, copper, stucco."

Virgilio Vespignani created the so-called Octagonal Hall, a wooden pavilion with elegant decorations inside the covered courtyard of the Palazzo dei Conservatori to house the most important sculptures discovered during that period. It was

General view
of the Octagonal Hall
created by Virgilio Vespignani

Following pages
The new layout of the gallery
of the *Horti Lamiani*

inaugurated in 1876, just a few years after excavations had begun. When the room was first opened there were 133 statues but during its twenty-seven year existence until it was demolished in 1903, an increasing number of works were placed in the Vespignani pavilion after being restored as excavation continued and new sculptures were constantly being discovered.

In 1903 the Museum of the Palazzo dei Conservatori acquired new spaces next to the internal garden that had once housed the Octagonal Hall and Rodolfo Lanciani, a key figure in Roman archaeology of that period, was in charge of their new arrangement, which divided them according to their origins. Today many of those works have been returned to the same hall but with a new arrangement that highlights the preciousness of the marbles and artistic quality of the ancient statues while respecting the museographical choices of the original arrangement.

A section of the "di Palombara" alabaster floor

Lesene capital
with inlaid colored marble

Jewels from elaborate room decorations

Halls of the Horti Lamiani I-III

"I saw a gallery that was 79 meters long, with a floor made of rare and expensive varieties of alabaster and a ceiling supported by 20 columns with ancient yellow fluting, resting on gilded plinths; I saw another room, with slabs of peacock butterfly, with walls covered with slate-black slabs, decorated with elegant arabesques in gold leaf; and finally, I saw a third room with a floor of alabaster segments enclosed in green vitreous pastes. On its walls there were various jets of water all around, each a meter apart and which were to meet in various ways, creating extraordinary light effects. All of these things were discovered in November 1875."

Thus Rodolfo Lanciani describes the extraordinary finds on the Esquiline, in the area between the current Piazza Vittorio Emanuele and Piazza Dante, and identified as pertinent to the ancient *Horti Lamiani* as a result of the study of literary sources. Originally, this magnificent villa belonged to a family that probably came from Formia, and that began its climb to political and social power in Rome with Lucius Aelius Lamia, reaching its height with a grandson of the same name, consul in 3 AD. As was the case for many other estates in the same area, very soon the *Horti Lamiani* became Imperial property, perhaps already under the principality of Tiberius. However, thanks to the testimony of Philon Alexandrinus who visited

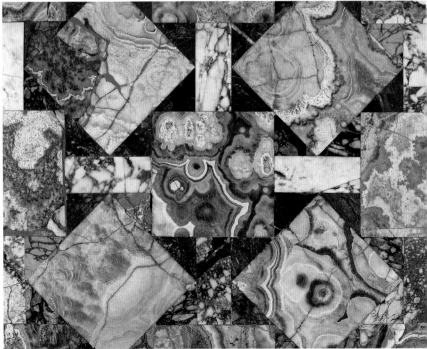

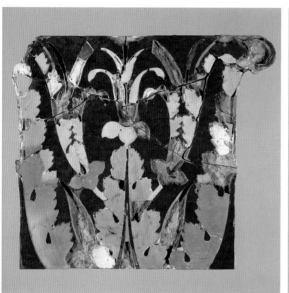
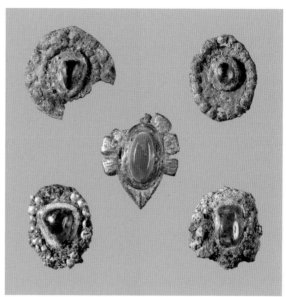

them in 38 AD, we know for sure that Caligula lived there and carried out extensive restoration on the existing buildings in the park so that the residence "would become even more splendid."

The structures discovered at the end of the nineteenth century include a magnificent nymphaeum in the form of a histrionic cavea overlooking a valley, a long portico overlooking rooms decorated with garden paintings and the magnificent complex described by Lanciani, consisting in the long criptoporticus and a series of spa-like rooms. Today, hidden by the modern city, none of this can be seen any longer. What does remain is the magnificent decorative and sculptural structure of the villa that was rediscovered during excavation and can once again be seen in the Palazzo dei Conservatori.

Amongst the most valuable objects on show in Hall I, some of which are Greek originals and are the fruit of a particular collector's style and the constant reference of Roman scholars to the artistic culture of the Classical age are two Greek funerary stelae from different periods and the group of the *ephedrismós* depicting two young girls playing on each other's shoulders.

What remains of the magnificent "di Palombara" alabaster floor (so-called by Roman marble workers because prior to the nineteenth-century urbanization Villa Palombara was located in this area), which decorated the around 80 meters long underground gallery, is a small section compared to its total area, on show in Hall II, and which still manages to convey the idea of the lavishness of the architectural decorations. Not far away, the splendid pilaster capitals in *opus sectile* were discovered where, on a red marble plinth, the decorative motifs are created with

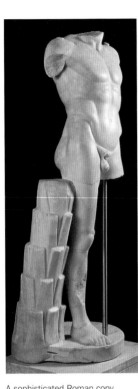

A sophisticated Roman copy
of Polycletus' Diadumenos

a valuable inlay of colored marble. "In the southern corner of Piazza Vittorio Emanuele, in the area of the ancient *Horti Lamiani*, the remains came to light of a piece of wooden furniture encrusted with gilded bronze, bucrania, festoons of fruit, fusaroles, candlesticks, pods. Gems such as cornelian, jasper, amethyst, garnet, onyx, cat's eye and lapis lazuli are set in each of the decorations. Some of the stones, in particular those with more than one layer, are engraved with animal figures, virile busts, etc. The feet of the piece of furniture are engraved in mountain crystal."
An initial analysis of this rich array of valuable materials led to the belief that this was a valuable piece of furniture which, after careful calculations includes: 296 agate plates, 441 set and loose gems, 28 of rock crystal fragments, 4 engraved gems, 3 set rock crystal plates, 40 fragments of amber, 1 fragment of small emerald plasma veneer, 1 small leaf in emerald plasma, an undefined number of lamina in gilded copper, both smooth and with embossed decorative motifs, a large number of nails, setting tubes, clamps and empty mountings.
In actual fact, they are probably the fragments of the lavish and garish decorations of a room, the walls of which were covered with wood decorated with this lamina of gilded metal, creating patterns that enclosed the gems and other decorative materials. The effect of this lavish pomp can be seen in the palatial decorations in paintings of the second Pompeian style.
During the Christmas period of 1874, an underground room was discovered with an extraordinary group of sculptures, which were removed to preserve them from imminent danger and were placed in Hall III. Thus, the beautiful Esquiline Venus was saved, depicted naked and putting up her hair while preparing for a bath, accompanied by two magnificent figures of priestesses or Muses with a treatment of the surfaces and clear stylistic analogies that makes them very similar to the main figure in the group, in particular in the faces with their sfumato outlines and porcelain-like flesh. These works go back to the first Imperial age and were inspired by Greek models from different periods, reflecting the eclectic taste that was typical of Roman art.
The beautiful group of sculptures depicting Emperor Commodus, shown as Hercules and with two marine creatures at his side, the Tritones, in a complex allegory symbolising the apotheosis of the emperor in his life was also discovered on the same site. As a result of his "excessive" behaviour, immediately after his death Commodus was subjected to the *damnatio memoriae*, a measure that meant the destruction of all his images and citations in official inscriptions: this might be the very reason for the concealment and, as a consequence, the preservation of this priceless sculpture. The statue of Dionysus lying down was also found in the same area, and was probably part of a larger group that must have also included other figures belonging to the retinue of the god.
The beautiful head of a Centaur and the statue of Diadumenus, an elegant copy from the Roman age of a famous and celebrated statue of Polycletus showing an athlete oiling himself, was also found in the *Horti Lamiani* area.

The deity is nude, seen as she is putting her hair up into an intricate hairstyle before bathing. The support beside her, on which she has placed a soft cloth, is made up of an Egyptian vase around which is coiled a cobra, and a small chest full of roses, perhaps to be used to add fragrance to her bath. These symbols suggest that the deity may have been intended as an Isis-Aphrodite, a religious synthesis elaborated in Hellenized Egypt.
The work, a creation from the

Roman period harking back to Greek models from different periods, is fascinating mainly because of the freshness of the modelling and the refined details.

The extraordinarily effective semi-feral aspect of the face and the exasperated expressive rendition of the tormented features make this head very similar to the Polyphemus group in Sperlonga, and especially that of Ulysses. Perhaps the commissioner himself (Tiberius, owner of the Villa di Sperlonga and heir to the property of the *Aelii Lamiae*) presided over the creation of this group of works, consciously harking back to the Hellenistic art of Rhodes and Pergamum.

Group of Commodus as Hercules flanked by two Tritons

The bust is one of the most famous masterpieces of Roman portraiture and depicts the emperor in the guise of Hercules, whose attributes he has been given: the lion's skin over his head, the club in his right hand, and the golden apples of Hesperides in his left hand as a reminder of the Greek hero's feats. The incredibly well-preserved bust is placed on a complex allegorical composition: two kneeling Amazons (only one is well-preserved) beside a globe decorated with the signs of the zodiac hold aloft a cornucopia which is entwined with a *pelta*, the Amazons' characteristic shield. The celebratory intent that, through a wealth of symbols, imposes the divine cult of the emperor, is further underlined by the two marine Tritons flanking the central figure to express his apotheosis. The group was recovered in an underground room of the *Horti Lamiani* complex, where it had probably been hidden.

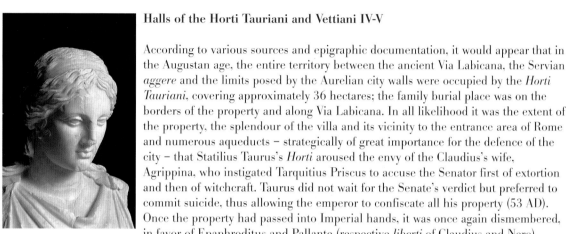

Bust of a female deity

Halls of the Horti Tauriani and Vettiani IV-V

According to various sources and epigraphic documentation, it would appear that in the Augustan age, the entire territory between the ancient Via Labicana, the Servian *aggere* and the limits posed by the Aurelian city walls were occupied by the *Horti Tauriani*, covering approximately 36 hectares; the family burial place was on the borders of the property and along Via Labicana. In all likelihood it was the extent of the property, the splendour of the villa and its vicinity to the entrance area of Rome and numerous aqueducts – strategically of great importance for the defence of the city – that Statilius Taurus's *Horti* aroused the envy of the Claudius's wife, Agrippina, who instigated Tarquitius Priscus to accuse the Senator first of extortion and then of witchcraft. Taurus did not wait for the Senate's verdict but preferred to commit suicide, thus allowing the emperor to confiscate all his property (53 AD). Once the property had passed into Imperial hands, it was once again dismembered, in favor of Epaphroditus and Pallante (respective *liberti* of Claudius and Nero), before being partially reunited under Gallienus (253-268 AD) in the *Horti Liciniani*. The remains of a building that, due to the names inscribed on the *fistulae aquariae* may refer to Vettius Agorius Praetextatus (*praefectus Urbi* in 367-368 AD) and his wife Fabia Aconia Paulina, were discovered in the western borders of the area. A wall discovered in the area and built with fragments of sculptures, as was verified in many other cases on the Esquiline, revealed an extraordinary amount of materials. The sculptures discovered in this area can be attributed to various phases in the life of the *horti*: in Hall IV, in particular the splendid statue of Hygeia; its style and dimensions make it similar to the bust of a female deity, recognisable as Artemis, the copy of an original, and attributed to Kephisodotos in the fourth century BC which was found nearby and probably belonged to the same group; a third statue with similar proportions was found in the same area and transformed in Christian Rome at the end of the nineteenth century to decorate the top of the Capitoline tower.
A setting inside a residence immersed in green seems to be particularly suitable for the works exhibited in Hall V: the statue of a cow, perhaps part of a pastoral group and probably a copy of the famous bronze statue of the same subject created by Myron for the Athens Acropolis and brought to Rome during the Vespasian age. The reliefs are also easy to place in the decoration of a garden. One, which is of particular elegance, depicts a sacred landscape with a sanctuary enclosed by high walls, while the other two, of which unfortunately only fragments remain, are neo-Attic artefacts which depict the quadriga of Helios (the sun) and Selene (the moon) running towards each other.
Further decorations of the villa gardens also include the two large amphorae decorated respectively with scenes of the Dionysian world and the marriage of Paris and Helen, while the splendid portraits of Hadrian, Sabina and Matidia, which were discovered during the demolition of the late-ancient walls of the *Horti Tauriani* in the gallery, must be attributed to the Imperial age.

Craters

The two craters are perfect
decorative objects for a garden,
and were probably used as basins
for a fountain. The two vases are
markedly different stylistically in
decorative terms: one is lively,
in keeping with the movement
expressed by the Dionysian dance;
the other is much more static, and
represents the marriage of Paris
and Helen according to the
stylemes of cold classicism.

Statue of Hygeia

This imposing larger-than-life-size
figure is of an elegantly draped
deity (probably Hygeia): the
mantle, resting on her left
shoulder, collects in a heavy,
plastic roll of folds on her
stomach.
A bracelet of twined threads
decorates her left wrist while, just
above her right elbow, there is a
precious armband studded with
an engraved jewel.
This is a late-Republican
re-elaboration of a fourth century
BC original.

Halls of the Horti of Maecenas VI-VIII

According to literary sources, the first person to colonize the Esquiline as a luxury residence was Maecenas, who completed the reclamation of the area that had previously been occupied by a millenary burial ground with a town planning intervention remembered by Horace. Indeed, the area of the ancient Esquiline burial ground was covered with a thick layer of earth that made it possible to transform a notorious area into a residential area of outstanding prestige. Constructed in the second half of the first century BC by this famous figure who was also friend and advisor of Augustus, the nineteenth-century excavations revealed few remains from this lavish residence: the only room that has been preserved is the so-called *Auditorium*, probably a semi-hypogeum summer triclinium decorated with frescoes in two stages: the first going back to 40 BC, attributable to the same Maecenas, while the second went back to the first decade AD when the villa had already become Imperial property. Unfortunately in very poor condition, the frescoes show views of the gardens with small sculptures and fountains, almost as if wanting to annul the lack of an opening to the outside of the large hall.

In the Neronian age, the villa that wound along the Servian walls, clearly no longer functional to the defence of the city, was a sort of continuation of the immense territorial expansion occupied by the *Domus Aurea*. And thus, the Imperial Palace was increasingly similar to the ones of Hellenistic sovereigns and expanded on the spaces available "specialising" the various building nuclei depending on their function: the area of the Palatine was for official purposes while the sectors of the Oppius and the Esquiline were known as villas of pleasure. The joke that went around Rome after the construction of the *Domus Aurea* and told by Suetonius is famous: "Rome will become his home: Migrate to Veii, Romans, as long as this house does not absorb Veii, too!" It would appear that Nero watched the spectacle of the burning of Rome from a tower on one of the highest sites of the *Horti* of Maecenas.

The reconstruction of the decorations of this residence has been extremely arduous since most of the sculptures that were found during excavations were reused as building material for the late-ancient or early-mediaeval walls.

In view of the interests of the villa proprietor, the finding of a series of herms with portraits attributable to figures of literary circles and exhibited in Hall VI are of particular importance: an existence that is of considerable significance in relation to the activities of Maecenas, who was well-known as a patron of the arts and in particular in relation to what we have found in literary sources on the sculptural decorations in the houses of the most famous figures. In the home of an intellectual (such as Maecenas) or a would-be intellectual, a library was a must, decorated with the images of the most famous Greek and Latin men of letters. In the decorative programme of this residence surrounded by greenery, the small reliefs with idyllic scenes and the elegant example of neo-Attic art of the *rhytòn*-shaped fountain signed by the artist Pontios, which corresponds perfectly to the beautiful relief with the dancing Maenad, a neo-Attic copy of the choral votive offering for the *Bacchants* of Euripides, created by Kallimachos in 406-405 BC all blend perfectly.

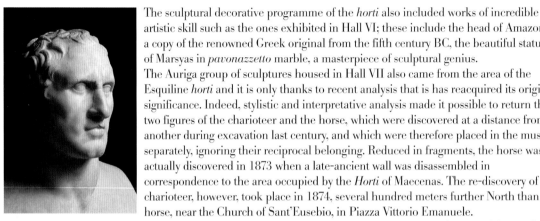

Poet's Herm

The sculptural decorative programme of the *horti* also included works of incredible artistic skill such as the ones exhibited in Hall VI; these include the head of Amazon, a copy of the renowned Greek original from the fifth century BC, the beautiful statue of Marsyas in *pavonazzetto* marble, a masterpiece of sculptural genius.

The Auriga group of sculptures housed in Hall VII also came from the area of the Esquiline *horti* and it is only thanks to recent analysis that is has reacquired its original significance. Indeed, stylistic and interpretative analysis made it possible to return the two figures of the charioteer and the horse, which were discovered at a distance from one another during excavation last century, and which were therefore placed in the museum separately, ignoring their reciprocal belonging. Reduced in fragments, the horse was actually discovered in 1873 when a late-ancient wall was disassembled in correspondence to the area occupied by the *Horti* of Maecenas. The re-discovery of the charioteer, however, took place in 1874, several hundred meters further North than the horse, near the Church of Sant'Eusebio, in Piazza Vittorio Emanuele.

Once again, the discovery was made during the disassembling of a wall of the "early Middle Ages," which had been built with thousand of sculptural fragments and many of the sculptures exhibited in the sector dedicated to the *Horti Tauriani* are the result of the recomposition of these.

Returned to its original form, the group of statues therefore depicts a naked male figure about to climb onto a cart drawn by two horses: the scene has been interpreted as the depiction of the abduction of Antiope, queen of the Amazons, by Theseus. Some of the marks on the male figure might indicate the presence of another person, Amazon herself who has been abducted, near the hero; however no traces were found in the Capitoline collections of this sculpture. From a stylistic point of view, the work would appear not to be a copy of a codified Greek model but rather a Roman age reinterpretation of Greek stylistic features of the fifth century BC.

In the ambit of the *Horti* of Maecenas the presence of some female statues identifiable as Muses, is also significant, mirroring the fame of the proprietor as patron of the arts and artists, while the Egyptian green marble sculpture of a guard dog is probably an example of cultivated collecting. The funerary stele exhibited in Hall VIII is both rare and valuable, an original Greek work showing a young girl wearing a complicated fabric in which the diverse qualities of the materials are highlighted with their accurate outlines in the dense folds; the right hand is extended and it appears that the left hand is lifting the folds of the chiton in the characteristic gesture of a late-Archaic *kore*. A work of considerable artistic skill, perhaps attributable to a place of worship in the gardens, is that of the colossal statue of Demeter, an elegant Roman copy from an original from the middle of the fifth century BC where the deliberate geometry of the folds of the fabric and the slight turn of the bust give the figure considerable internal tension.

While the Olympian splendour of the deity is highlighted in this work, the statue of Hercules fighting is characterized by the dynamism, depicting him in animated movement and based on Greek models from the fourth century BC.

According to Greek myth, the Phrygian Marsyas, after coming across Athena's aulos, or flute, dared challenge Apollo to a musical competition. Through various ruses, Apollo won the contest, judged by the Muses, but sought his revenge on Marsyas, who had dared challenge a god: Marsyas was flayed alive and his skin hung from a pine tree. The statue, a Roman copy of a Hellenistic original, deftly exploits the veins of the *pavonazzetto* marble to render the flayed body: the odd position of the figure with its tensed musculature and suffering face, a masterpiece of "expressionistic art," inspired many representations of the crucifixion.

This is a fragment of a statue of extraordinary quality, and specifically the head of an Amazon. It is a copy of an original bronze made for a competition in Ephesus between 444 and 430 BC. The greatest artists of the period participated in the competition, including Kresilas, Pheidias, Polycletus and an otherwise unknown sculptor by the name of Phradmon. Polycletus was declared the winner, as each participant came second to himself.

Dog

The imposing size and vigilant aspect seem to link this figure of a dog with those commonly placed outside Roman homes. However in this case, considering the expensive, rare green marble from Egypt (*serpentina moschinata*, according to the denomination of the Roman marble-workers), worked with extraordinary deftness and the characteristic race of the animal, it seems that the sculpture can be attributed to Alexandrian production and considered a precious collectable artistic object to be set in the *Horti* of Maecenas.

The Pontios Rhytòn

On a goblet formed of undulated leaves there is a drinking horn tapering into the body of a winged gryphon and decorated with a string of dancing Maenads along the rim. The fountain, an extremely refined example of decorative art from the neo-Attic school, is signed by the Greek artist Pontios and was found in the area of the *Horti* of Maecenas.

In this unfortunately fragmentary figure, the Muse of Tragedy is depicted with her bust leaning forward and left foot lifted and resting on a little rocky mound. This peculiar position generates an elegant design in the heavy cloth drapery, which is set out according to a refined, curvilinear design.
Tied around her waist is a *nebride*, a goatskin typically used by characters from the Dionysian sphere and harking back to the origins of tragedy. The statue is a re-elaboration of a fourth century BC Greek original, and was found in the *Horti* of Maecenas.

The figure is thrusting forward in a forcefully dynamic gesture. The tension of the body, accentuated by the careful anatomical study of the muscular structure and the intensely concentrated facial expression underline the aggression linked to the impetus of combat. The work, which is a copy of an original Greek bronze from the late fourth century BC, was found in many different fragments, and was used as construction material for a wall in the *Horti* of Maecenas.

View of the roofing
and the interior of the Exhedra
of Marcus Aurelius

The Exhedra of Marcus Aurelius

The new large glass hall built inside what was once known as the "Roman Garden" of the Palazzo dei Conservatori shows, in chronological order, the last, prestigious architectural creation in the Capitoline Museum complex. The aim of the project, created by Carlo Aymonino, was the creation of an ample luminous space that represented the heart of the museum, to enhance the extraordinary monumental appearance of the Temple of Capitoline Jupiter and to represent the heart of the exhibition between the historic part of the Palazzo dei Conservatori with the official, frescoed rooms of the Apartment, and the more recently built sections of the museum, located inside the ancient Caffarelli property. The drafting of the project took many years and included the conception of various solutions that gradually took into consideration not only the perfectioning of the aesthetic and architectural value of the intervention itself, but also the novelties and discoveries that were made during this decade. In its architectural capacity and in the drafting of the exhibition contents, the project therefore developed "historically," without changing the original needs but rather shaping them in relation to the renewed needs and "function" of the exhibition, as a valuable container for the conservation and exaltation of the majestic remains of the Temple of Capitoline Jupiter. The architectural intervention was carried out within an outdoor area which, in the past,

The equestrian statue
of Marcus Aurelius

marked the boundary between the property of the Conservators and the Caffarelli family: the first archive documentation to mention this space goes back to the beginning of the sixteenth century, to the same period in which this family began to consolidate its presence in Capitoline Hill with the construction of the first wing of its palace. The maps and views of Rome make it possible to follow the architectural evolution of the property, the history of which is almost inextricably interwoven with that of the Palazzo dei Conservatori. In 1876, in this very same space (called the "kitchen garden" of the Palazzo dei Conservatori) an octagonal pavilion with an elegant modern design was built on a project by Virgilio Vespignani, to house the great sculptural remains from the excavations linked to the urbanization of new quarters after the proclamation of Rome as capital. Today, the large, luminous hall, with the latest technology, heir of that prior creation, houses the great equestrian statue of Marcus Aurelius. After restoration on the work had been completed in the nineties, the technicians were strongly against it being exhibited outdoors in its original position, as this would have compromised its conservation. The decision was therefore taken to create a faithful copy of the sculpture, which had already been in the center of the piazza for years, and to place the original inside, in a "protected" environment. Marcus Aurelius, the highest Capitoline symbol, therefore represents the heart of the new exhibition, around which the most important archaeological testimonies regarding ancient Capitoline Hill and some of the great bronzes, the "primordial" nucleus of the Capitoline collections of antiquity all gravitate in a particularly evocative and suggestive exhibition.

Equestrian statue of Marcus Aurelius

There is no mention of the equestrian statue dedicated to the Emperor Marcus Aurelius (161-180 AD) in ancient literary sources, but it was in all likelihood erected in 176 AD, along with numerous other honors on the occasion of his triumph over the Germanic tribes, or in 180 AD soon after his death. There were many equestrian statues in Rome at that time: late-Imperial descriptions of the areas of the city listed 22 such statues, called *equi magni*, that is larger-than-life-size, just like the monument to Marcus Aurelius. The latter statue, however, is the only one to have survived to the present, and by virtue of its integrity it soon assumed symbolic value for all those who wished to present themselves as heirs to Imperial Rome. We do not know where the statue was originally displayed. However, Carlo Fea, who was the first to attribute the statue's survival to the fact that it was mistaken for a statue of Constantine, refused to accept the hypothesis put forward by Nardini, and accepted by Winckelmann, that the statue was originally erected at the Lateran, where it was recorded in mediaeval sources. In fact, all we can affirm is that the statue was erected as a public dedication and that, therefore, its original location was most probably the Roman Forum or the square with the dynastic temple that surrounded the Antonine Column.

Its location in the Lateran is first recorded in the tenth century, but it is likely that it had been there from at least the end of the eighth century, when Charlemagne wanted to copy the layout of *Campus Lateranensis* when he transferred a similar equestrian statue, taken from Ravenna, to his palace in Aachen.

In January 1538, Pope Paul II ordered the Farnese family to have the statue moved to the Capitoline Hill, which had become the headquarters of the city's authorities in 1143. A year after its arrival, the Roman Senate commissioned Michelangelo to refurbish the statue. The great Florentine artist did not just limit himself to planning an appropriate site for the monument, but made it the central element in the magnificent architectural complex known as the piazza of the Capitoline Hill.

Local government inspection undertaken after the terrorist attack near the Palazzo Senatorio on April 19, 1979, revealed that the equestrian statue of Marcus Aurelius was severely corroded and that its statics were worrying, mainly due to the chinks and cracks found in the horse's legs. On January 8, 1981, the horseman was removed from Michelangelo's base, and on January 17 the monument was moved to a workshop at the Istituto Centrale per il Restauro. As there were no established procedures for the conservation of statues of this sort, undertaking restoration allowed the team to develop innovative analytical and technological techniques.

After a very carefully undertaken preliminary study, which aimed to define the state of the bronze statue and how to intervene, restoration work was concluded at the end of 1988, and the equestrian monument took out a new lease of life. The structural and surface fragility of the bronze statue brought to experts' attention the theme of protecting masterpieces that are not housed in museums.

It was soon clear that it would be possible to protect the statue adequately only if it were sheltered from the vagaries of the weather to which it had been subjected in the open air.

And although everyone wanted to see the bronze statue put back in its central position in the piazza of the Capitoline Hill, it was responsibly decided that this could not be done.

The only choice that could be made was to provisionally accomodate the statue in a carefully controlled indoor space; in this way the statue could be

preserved while at the same time the unique, invaluable artefact could be made available to the general public.

On April 11, 1990, the monument was returned to the piazza of the Capitoline Hill and was placed in the Capitoline Museum courtyard, where it was placed in a large glass case.

This left the primary concern of how to restore the unity of Michelangelo's project. It was therefore decided to make a copy of the original. For various reasons, it was not possible to adopt the two traditional techniques of a direct mold or using a compass and pantograph to chart an exact replica. The former was impossible because of the parlous state of the residual gilding, which was peeling away from the bronze base; the latter because it would have been impossible to faithfully reproduce all the quirks of the original, plastic form, which had accrued during its long history. It was therefore decided to undertake a so-called "indirect" procedure where the geometric form would be reproduced thanks to a digital model obtained by means of a "photogrametric" survey. The "skin" would then be integrated manually through the use of craftsmanlike techniques.

In 1997, technicians from the State mint completed the bronze copy, and on April 19 of the same year it was placed on Michelangelo's original base at the center of the piazza on the Capitoline Hill.

At the same time the copy was being made, authorities dealt with the problem of housing the original in a more permanent museum space. An appropriate place, in terms of size and dignity, was found within the Capitoline Museums, and restructuring was begun in 1997.

With this in mind, a new pavilion was planned in the Roman Garden on the first floor of the Palazzo dei Conservatori, where, soon after the unification of Italy in the nineteenth century, most of the statues discovered after excavations were undertaken for the capital's new districts were housed.

The glass enclosure for the garden, undertaken by the architect Carlo Aymonino, was considered the most appropriate solution, and the equestrian monument would be joined by other important bronze works from the Capitoline collection that were also part of the *pignora imperii* held at the Lateran since the Middle Ages and moved to the Capitoline Museums at the end of the fifteenth century with the aim of giving the Roman people tangible proof of the ancient dignity of the hill.

The new base, designed by the architect Francesco Stefanori and undertaken, along with the statue's berth, by the Centro di Ricerca Scienza e Tecnica per la Conservazione del Patrimonio Storico-Architettonico (CISTeC) of the University of Rome "La Sapienza", was purposefully different from Michelangelo's original pedestal, both in order to avoid any form of comparison and to underline the difference between the equestrian statue's original open-air location and its current enclosure within the museum.

Needless to say, the new pavilion, which was built bearing in mind the monumental relics from the Temple of Capitoline Jupiter, not only offers a specific and definitive solution to the problem of the bronze statue of Marcus Aurelius, but also constitutes the focal point (in keeping with such works in other European museums) for the overall enhancement of the Capitoline Museums and the entire Capitoline Hill.

Gilded bronze statue of Hercules

The statue originated in the Forum Boarium, where it was found during the pontificate of Sixtus IV. The statue must have represented the cult statue within the round temple dedicated to the Greek hero in the second century BC. The statue's proportions and strong modeling demonstrate that it was based on Greek models of the fourth century BC, close to the Lysippic style.
A recent hypothesis suggests that it could have derived directly from the mold of a bronze statue of that period.

Beginning in the mediaeval period, the precious remains of the sculpture depicting the first Christian emperor – the head, hand, and globe – were part of the patrimony of the patriarch's Lateran residence. In 1471, they went to the Capitoline Hill, as part of Sixtus IV's donation to the People of Rome.

The large head, a masterpiece of antique bronze statuary, impressive both in the colossal scale and the intensity of the features, has been associated with portraits of Constantine during the last period of his life. The hand originally meant to hold the globe, a symbol of power over the world, is generally attributed to the statue.

A view of the area
of the Temple of Jupiter

The Temple of Capitoline Jupiter

In the most ancient history of Rome, the sixth century BC corresponds to the reign of
the Etruscan dynasty of the Tarquins, a period that was marked by the expansion of the
city and their dominion in Latium and by the creation of important works of public
building. During a battle against the Sabines, Tarquinius Priscus (616-579 BC), the fifth
king of Rome and the first of the Etruscan dynasty, dedicated a temple to Jupiter
Optimus Maximus, Juno and Minerva in exchange for victory. Thus began the layout of
the area chosen on Monte Tarpeo, flattening the western peak of the hill and
constructing an enclosing wall. The son Tarquinius Superbus continued the project that
had been interrupted but without managing to complete it since he was ousted from
Rome following a general revolution against the monarchy. It was not until the first year
of the Roman Republic, on September 13, 509 BC that the temple was consecrated by
Consul Horatius Pulvillus.
According to historians, small buildings of worship already existed on the site of the
temple. The wishes of the respective divinities were therefore studied and almost all
agreed that the sacellum should be moved and dedicated to them: only *Terminus* and
Juventas refused and their altars remained inside the new temple. Amongst the various
legends pertaining to the construction of the temple, there is also one saying that during
the excavations of the foundations of the new building, a perfectly preserved human
skull was found, and this prodigy was taken as a sign that the hill, called *Capitolium* ever
since, was to become the center of power of Imperial Rome.
Situated in a commanding position, the Temple of Jupiter, Juno and Minerva, was
recognized as the sanctuary of the protective divinities of the city and as such it also
had to be perceived by nearby Etruria and the Latin peoples who had their common
religious center in the Sanctuary of *Iuppiter Latiaris* on Monte Cavo.
All that remains of the large building the Tarquin family desired is just part of the
imposing foundations in gossan blocks. Although it was systematically destroyed in the
post-Antique age and used as a quarry for valuable materials, today the extraordinary
dimensions of the temple are still astounding even though it no longer has its original
façade or rich architectural decorations. Following a violent fire (83 BC) it was destroyed
in the first century BC and we know that it was rebuilt on the same foundations and with
the same measurements of the Archaic one, using, according to a literary source, the
columns in Pentelic marble taken from the Athens *Olympieion*. In view of the absence of
hard evidence, both the description by Dionysus of Halicarnassus and the comments by
the architect Vitruvius are of great value for the reconstruction of the first building. The
temple was built on an extremely high podium and was around 200 feet long (that is, 60
meters); its width was a little shorter than its length. It faced south and had three rows of
columns on the façade and one on each side. It had three parallel cellas, separated by
walls but covered by the same roof: the central one was dedicated to Jupiter, those on the
sides to Juno and Minerva. The temple floor, which was much higher than the current
one in the museum area, was at around the height of the Caffarelli terrace we see today.

Perspectival view of the wall
in blocks of outcrop stone
from the podium of the Temple
of Capitoline Jupiter, the so-called
"Roman Wall," surmounted
by a plan of the building
in *opus caementicium*

Vitruvius adds that the columns were very far from one another: it was therefore an
aerostyle temple. Typical of Tuscan temples, this characteristic did not permit the use of
stone architraves, which would have been too heavy for such a wide opening, but only
ones of wood. Indeed, the reconstructable intercolumniation on the basis of the
preserved structures shows that the central one was 12.50 meters while the lateral ones
measured 8 meters. The colossal dimensions of the Capitoline Temple (62 m. x 54 m.)
can be appreciated better if compared to other coeval temples. For example, the Temple
of the Sacred area of the Forum Boarium measured 10.60 m. x 10.60 m., and that of
Portonaccio in Veii 18.50 m. x 18.50 m.

We know from historic sources that Tarquinius Priscus commissioned Vulca, coroplasta
of Veii, the religious statue in terracotta dedicated to Jupiter. The god was depicted
standing up and with a thunderbolt in his right hand; during certain festivities his face
was colored red. Other artists from Veii were commissioned with the large terracotta
quadriga that was to hang over the roof. As regards the latter, it is said that during firing,
instead of losing water the artefact increased in volume so much that it actually burst the
kiln it was in. The bishops interpreted this wonder as an omen of the future power of
Rome. All that remains of the Archaic age temple are parts of the majestic foundations:

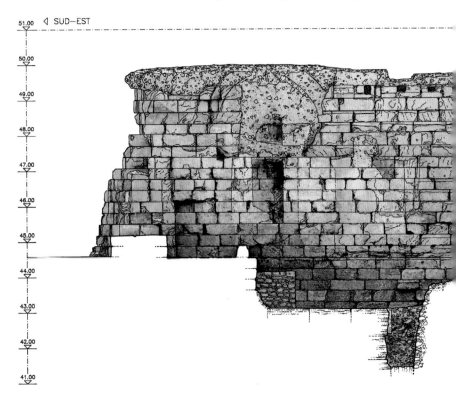

the building was completely rebuilt no less than four times in the Roman age; furthermore, from ancient writers we know that the decorative elements that had been ruined or were to be replaced were buried in the swamps since they were considered sacred. For these reasons the decorations can only be reconstructed on the basis of a comparison with coeval buildings. It is likely that the columns were in plastered travertine, that the walls of the cella and the door stiles were decorated with plates of painted silver. On the façade the roof must have had an open tympanum, in side of which one could see the heads of the *columen* and the *mutuli* covered by slabs of terracotta with diverse decorations. Both the roof weathering and the cover below must have had panes decorated with floral motifs, alternating small palms and lotus flowers, fretworked sima and shrouds, while along the long sides the edges of the roof were decorated with antefixa, perhaps in the shape of the heads of Silenus and a Maenad. The history of the Temple of Capitoline Jupiter is inextricably interwoven with the expansion of Roman imperialism: all the rites prior to a departure of conquest took place in the Capitoline sanctuary, and the triumphal processions conceded to the victorious generals by the Senate all took place in the Temple of Jupiter. It soon became the symbol of the city of Rome and as such was reproduced in all the new cities that were founded.

NORD—OVEST ▷ 51.00

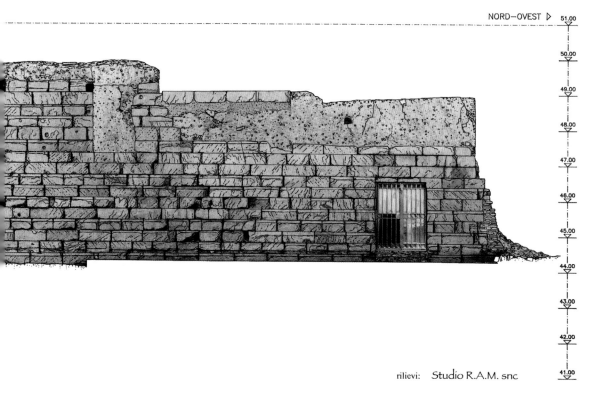

50.00

49.00

48.00

47.00

46.00

45.00

44.00

43.00

42.00

rilievi: Studio R.A.M. snc

41.00

Reconstruction of the stages
of life as identified during
archaeological surveys conducted
in the Roman Garden
(illustration Inklink, Florence).
From left to right: site of the
Temple of Jupiter (sixth century
BC); Archaic-oriental buildings
(seventh-sixth century BC);
Early Iron Age (tenth-eighth
century BC); Bronze Age
(seventeenth-eleventh century BC)

Wounded warrior

The extant part of this work allows us to reconstruct a polychrome terracotta group dramatically representing a battle scene in which a warrior, perhaps an Amazon, has been wounded and brought down by an opponent, as can be evinced from Patricia S. Lulof's depiction. The figure is wearing Attic-style armour over a light tunic that elegantly falls over his left shoulder, and is bearing a cuirass, shield and jambeaux.

The sculpture, in full relief, was assembled over an internal, rough terracotta structure and covered with a layer of very fine clay. This allowed for an extremely refined modelling and extraordinary descriptive precision of the painted ornamental motifs.

The masterful use of color reaches its highest *pathos* in the realistic rendition of the open chest wound with the blood flowing over the cuirass and trickling over his body. Perhaps by Greek artists working in Rome in the early fifth century BC, this group, probably used to decorate the Esquiline Temple, was placed at the summit of the roof and constituted the central acroterium.

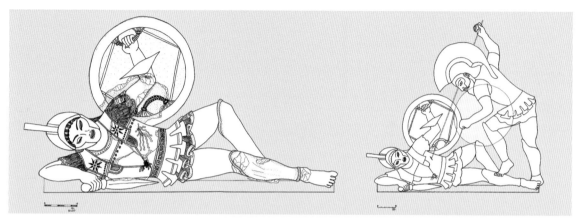

The Archaic Temple of the Sacred area of the Forum Boarium

Small ivory plate inscribed
with leonine forms, perhaps
a card exchanged as tangible sign
of reciprocal hospitality

Hypothetical reconstruction
of the Archaic Temple
of the Sacred area
of the Forum Boarium

On the slopes of the Capitoline Hill near the Tiber, near the sixteenth century Church of Sant'Omobono, around the middle of the twentieth century a temple building was discovered, referable to the last period of the Roman monarchy (sixth century BC).
Of this temple, which was probably dedicated to *Mater Matuta*, a deity identified with Aurora and protector of births, the structures of the podium were discovered 6 meters below the modern level, as were the remains of the cella walls in untreated clay and part of the polychrome terracotta decoration from the tympanum and the upper part of the roof.
In the original building, attributable to the first Tarquinius (616-579 BC), or as tradition will have it, to Servius Tullius (578-534 BC) – author of the urban rearrangement of the Forum Boarium and of the dedication in this area of the temples of Fortuna and *Mater Matuta* – the temple was characterized by the presence of a Corinthian type pediment decoration which is the oldest and unique example of a closed pediment in Etruscan-Italic architecture in the Archaic age: all that remains of this pediment decoration are two feline figured plaques and part of a Gorgon.
However, the remains of the reconstruction carried out by Tarquinius Superbus (534-509 BC) include the tiles with the processions of carts, the large volutes on the roof weathering, the Sphinxes in function of the lateral acroteria and the statues on the top

0   0,5   1   2   3   4   5 metri

Ipotesi ricostruttiva: Anna Mura Sommella - Germano Foglia

Acroterial group in painted
terracotta from the Archaic Temple
of the Forum Boarium

of the roof, as documented in the contemporary temples of Veii and Satricum. The most complete example of these sculptures in polychrome terracotta is the group, which was used as a central acroterium, depicting Athena presenting Heracles to Olympus.

The building was destroyed at the end of the sixth century BC, perhaps intentionally and violently, coinciding with the end of the monarchy and the beginning of the Republic. This important sacred building was reconstructed immediately, next to a twin temple, on extensive foundations that had been raised by around six meters compared to Archaic times, to avoid damage caused by the constant floods from the Tiber.

A store of *ex voto* referable to the entire life of the sanctuary in the sixth century was found in the rear of the Archaic Temple. The objects dedicated to the deity consisted in small vases produced locally and made of impasto and bucaro, valuable pottery imported from Greece and the East, objects referable to the world of women such as spindles, bunches of staples and pendants. Due to its rarity, a small ivory lion with an Etruscan inscription is of particular interest, datable between the end of the seventh and the beginning of the sixth century BC.

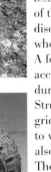

The most recent archaeological finds on the Capitoline Hill

According to ancient historic tradition, Rome was founded by Romulus in 754-753 BC; prior to this event, the site was inhabited by diverse populations – Siculans, early inhabitants of Latium, Pelasgians, Greeks, etc. – and, even earlier than these, by divinities who founded cities: Janus on Janiculus and Saturn on Capitoline Hill. Very detailed archaeological studies carried out in the area of the Roman Garden, together with the Istituto di Paletnologia of the University of Rome "La Sapienza" and the Archaeological Superintendency of Rome, have resulted in the concrete testimony of the presence of a settlement on the Capitoline Hill from the middle of the Bronze Age, the period from which numerous pottery fragments have been discovered. The analysis of the study results is still underway by the archaeologists who carried out the work.

A fenced in area on the hill slope with extensive works of terracing and an accumulation of pottery and animal bone confirm the continuity of the settlement during the thirteenth-twelfth century BC.

Structures created on the area with shattered materials as well as the presence of griddles are evidence of the use of the area at the end of the Bronze Age, the period to which a combustion structure that might have been a smelting kiln for metals is also to be attributed.

The characteristic clay soil that was well suited to the creation of the first, rudimental combustion structures, the dense woods on the hill that guaranteed the material needed, the nearby ford of the Tiber that facilitated trade certainly all led to the choice of this place for processing metals. Indeed, there is evidence of its use as such for a long period, until the Archaic age.

During the Iron Age, the area in question, which was evidently near a village, was used as a burial ground, in particular for infants, children and adolescents.

Four tombs from the early Iron Age were discovered there, two of which were of females, with lavish vase and personal objects (tomb no. 4 and no. 15); some of the vases contained offerings of food. Two large dolia placed horizontally contained infant remains.

Two tombs of young children are referable to the third Latian period while other remains, one in a chest and the others in a hollow, or rather in earthen jars or *tegulae* go back to somewhere between the end of the seventh and the beginning of the sixth century BC.

In this last period, some of the stone foundations, abundant pieces of tiles and pottery fragments are the last evidence of this settlement that was to be obliterated by the grandiose works for the construction of the Temple of Jupiter, Juno and Minerva.

Terracotta antefixus
in the form of a female head,
late sixth century BC,
from the digs
of the Roman Garden

Detail of the tempera decoration
of the socle of one of the rooms,
with anthropomorphic
and decorative elements

Palazzo Clementino Caffarelli

The restructuring of the Capitoline complex, which was started in the year 2000,
made it possible to include the entire building complex of the Palazzo Caffarelli
in the museum itinerary, also including the most ancient nucleus known as the
Palazzo Clementino.

There is abundant evidence, both documentary and iconographic, of the presence
in Capitoline Hill next to the Palazzo dei Conservatori of the property of one of the
most important Roman noble families, the Caffarelli. The Caffarelli property was
situated on the top of the hill in the area known as Monte Tarpeo, bordering the
area of the internal garden of the Palazzo dei Conservatori. Beginning in 1563, the
year in which the ground was levelled with the permission of the Capitoline
magistracy, the Caffarelli family carried out extensive work, creating a garden in the
shape of an open terrace overlooking the city and had an entrance portal to their
property erected; the date 1584 and the name Giovan Pietro were then inscribed.
These interventions can still be seen in Sallustio Peruzzi's *Map of Rome* in 1568.
Once the land had been regularized, the Caffarelli family, first Ascanio and then the
son Giovan Pietro began work on the construction of a small palace, the entrance of
which was straight after the portal. The building is closely linked to the Palazzo dei
Conservatori, partially overlooking the public courtyard on the right-hand side and
expanding in line with the lateral façade of the palace along Via delle Tre Pile.
The new building can be seen clearly on the map of Rome engraved by Antonio
Tempesta in 1593, while the name of the architect mentioned in seventeenth-
century sources, Gregorio Caronica, referable to the circle of Giacomo della Porta,
who continued the work of Michelangelo in the Capitoline Hill, is evidence of the
link with the contemporary Capitoline buildings.
In the first decade of the seventeenth century Giovan Pietro extended the palace on the
right-hand side of the Palazzo dei Conservatori. It was during the seventeenth century
that the body of the building reached the dimensions of the area that is now known as
the Palazzo and Giardino Caffarelli. Despite its new grandeur, the building, which was
now also covering the foundations of the Temple of Capitoline Jupiter, still appeared
disjointed, so much so that in the 1763 edition of the guide by Titi it was described as
being "of noble magnificence although unfinished." During the nineteenth century the
property passed into the hands of Prussia and the Palazzo Caffarelli underwent
considerable transformation when the Prussian embassy was established in the Papal
State and further events completely changed the internal structure of the palace. The
most ancient wing, the Palazzo Clementino, was given to the Municipality at the end of
the nineteenth century, becoming the headquarters of the administrative offices. This
new function led to a change in the distribution of the interior with the construction of
partitions and the opening of new corridors. These changes seriously damaged the
decorations of the rooms: tempera frescoes were completely covered while the wooden
ceilings suffered damage that can still be seen today.

Hall of the Frescoes
(or of Saint Peter), remnants
of a frescoed scene identified
as *The Miracle of Saint Peter*

In 1919 the Commission appointed to study the arrangement of the Capitoline Hill had the first archaeological excavations carried out in the wing of the palace built on top of the temple foundations, rediscovering the remains that were visible in many rooms such as the "passage way with Roman Wall" that linked the palace to the stables built on the opposite side of the garden. This work led to the almost total loss of the original rooms of the Palazzo Caffarelli.

The restoration carried out in these years concentrated mainly on the rooms of the most ancient nucleus, the so-called Palazzo Clementino. The original dimensions of the rooms were restored and ample parts of the decorations were retrieved, which had been covered up by various coats of paint and had thus been forgotten. Today, in all probability evidence of what the actual decorations of the main floor of the palace were like can be seen in the frescoes in the Hall of Saint Peter and the wall decorations in the adjoining rooms. Due to both its size and the richness of decorations, most of which have unfortunately been lost, the Hall of Saint Peter is one of the most important rooms. It is a complex perspective structure with columns, cornices and geometric divisions with great scenes depicted on the walls and smaller landscapes above the doors. A perimetrical frieze in which male faces alternated in geometrical intervals ran below the ceiling. Of the two scenes that have survived, one is the scene that gives the room its name: in front of the Temple of Jerusalem, Saint Peter is heeling a cripple.

The Capitoline Medal Collection

With a total of 50,000 pieces, the Capitoline Medal Collection, constituted in 1872, contains the numismatic, medal, glyptic and jewellery collections of the Municipal patrimony. With his donation of 9,074 coins of different origins, it was thanks to Augusto Castellani, a member of the famous Roman family of goldsmiths as well as director of the Capitoline Museums in 1873 that this new museum sector was created.

Castellani also bequeathed the necklace with a tiny mosaic medallion, which he had created in 1869 for the last Senator of Rome, Marquis Francesco Cavalletti Rondinini.

Three jewels designed
in the Castellani family
goldsmith workshop

Bejewelled choker containing
47 emeralds, 62 rubies and
76 sapphires; in the center:
minute mosaic madallion,
by Luigi Podio. The choker was
created in 1869 for the last
Roman Senator, the Marquis
Francesco Cavalletti Rondinini

Two *demi-parures*;
one in gold, the other in gold
and pearls, once belonging
to Giannina Fabri Speranza, last
direct descendent of the
Castellani family; donated by her
husband, Umberto Speranza, to
the Municipality of Rome in 1976

Purchases and excavations by the Archaeological Commission (1872-1925)
After the Unification of Italy and the proclamation of Rome as capital, the city
underwent intense urban restructuring that led to the excavation and destruction
of numerous areas that had previously been unbuilt. It was with the purpose of
supervising these archaeological discoveries and to receive the valuable information
on the finds being made in the area in question that a nucleus of archaeological
and collector experts, and members of the Municipal Council founded the
Archaeological Commission. It was thanks to this Commission and Camillo Serafini,
the first conservator of the Medal Collection, that large collections such as the
Campana, Bignami and Orsi were purchased and added to the Stanzani and
Castellani nuclei together with other smaller purchases. However, it was mainly
from the archaeological excavations in the areas foreseen for public buildings that
the most plentiful and abundant coin finds were made, mainly in bronze and less
frequently in silver and gold, as in the case of the Esquiline storeroom.

The excavations by the Governorship (1925-1939)
In October 1925 the Governorship of Rome was founded to replace the Municipal
Council. This new administrative structure, which was created to allow closer
coordination between the central fascist government and the peripheral
headquarters, thus considerably extended its power of action to the heart of cultural
activities. The Governorship was given all the finds from the demolishment of
entire quarters, such as those on the Capitoline Hill and those adjacent to Via dei

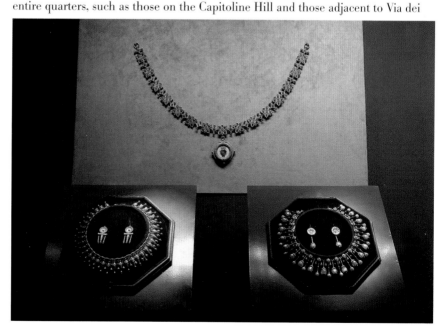

Fori Imperiali. In particular, during the intervention for the construction of the Gallery Junction of Capitoline palaces the small treasure of the Capitoline Hill was discovered, while in the one of the opening of Via dei Fori Imperiali the treasure of Via Alessandrina was unearthed.
Other significant finds of the same period are those of the treasure of the Torre delle Milizie, the nucleus of Republican *denarii* from the Sacred area of Largo Argentina and a group of "*contorniati*" found in the Forum of Augustus.

Purchases and donations in the second half of the twentieth century
After the Second World War the numismatic cabinet expanded as a result of several donations such as those by Di Castro (Republican asses and "madonnine" of Bologna) and Jordanov, and some rare and careful purchases made by the director of the Capitoline Museums, Carlo Pietrangeli and the successive conservator of the Medal Collection, Franco Panvini Rosati.
It also houses the complete series of the yearly coinage of the three medals, ordered by none other than the Municipality of Rome from the State Mint in celebration of the birthday of Rome and in conjunction with particular events such as the bestowing of decorations.
In 1976, in memory of his wife Giannina Fabri Speranza, descendant of Augusto Castellani, Umberto Speranza bequeathed the Capitoline Medal Collection two *demi-parures* made in gold and pearls by the workshop of the Castellani goldsmiths. In 1994 the Association "Friends of the Museums of Rome" made a magnificent gift of the sulphur casts of ancient gems from the Boncompagni Collection.

Exhibition itinerary

Castellani Donation
In 1872 the Stanzani Collection was bequeathed to a generic "Archaeological Cabinet of Rome" and since the only collection that might have expected to purchase the legacy at that time was the Vatican Medal Collection, Augusto Castellani decided to donate 9,074 coins to the Capitoline Museum, thus resulting in the creation of the Capitoline Medal Collection.
From the minutes attached to the resolution proposal presented before the Municipal Council of Rome, it appears that the donation consisted in 9,074 coins, 4,598 of which came from the excavations of Porto, while 2,700 were Imperial coins from the third and fourth century from Roman territory and a further 656 with the same origins were from the twelfth-fourteenth century.
The 42 pieces of libral *aes grave*, were presumably found in a treasure or rather in a votive storeroom discovered on the "Vatican Hills."

Book-shaped box containing
the Stanzani Collection of agates

Castellani Jewellery

The jewels, a choker with gems and two *demi-parures* were created in the goldsmith workshop of the Castellani family. They became part of the Capitoline Medal Collection at different times and in different ways. The pertinent documentation, a sketch book, precious manuscripts and registers of the workshop activity, together with a comparison with the significant legacy of precious stones to the Museum of Villa Giulia made it possible to date the jewels with accuracy and to shed further light on the activities of this important family of Roman goldsmiths and jewellers. The choker of the Senator of Rome is a lavish piece of jewellery commissioned in 1869 to Augusto Castellani together with the mosaicist Lugi Podio, for the last Senator of Rome, Francesco Cavalletti Rondinini, who governed the city until September 20, 1870. It is made of a large band of gold with elements in the shape of the cross of Saint Andrew and a Greek cross with the addition of rubies, emeralds and sapphires. On the right of the pendent is a tiny mosaic of the coat of arms of the Roman Senate, enclosed in a crown of oak in gold relief and on the back is an inscription in gold. The two *demi-parures* in gold belonged to a direct descendant of the Castellani family, Giannina Fabri Speranza, and were recovered and purchased back after the Second World War. Following her death, her husband Umberto Speranza donated them to the Capitoline Medal Collection in 1976 in her memory. The necklace with small filigree amphora, inspired by early Hellenism Greek goldsmiths and the earrings, which are similar but not a perfect match, were created by Castellani between 1875 and 1881. The gold necklace with pendants in baroque pearls and a pair of earrings in the same style with a disc and single pendent, created by Augusto Castellani in 1875, probably belonged to a princess of the Savoia family.

Stanzani Donation
In 1872 the architect Ludovico Stanzani died in Kiev, bequeathing his collection of 9,251 coins and 681 precious stones to the "Archaeological Cabinet of Rome." To make sure the Stanzani Collection went to the Capitoline Museums, Augusto Castellani decided to found the Capitoline Medal Collection and made the first donation. It was not until 1874 that the Municipality of Rome purchased the collection and had a concise inventory drawn up through the Municipal Archaeological Commission. This indexing was an extremely laborious process: very often the material was enclosed in small sheet of paper or in cards with brief notes in Russian. The number of mint in the numismatic collection varied greatly, with ancient pieces from Greek cities, Roman Republics, imperial and provincial, Byzantine and Mediaeval and modern Arabian, German, Russian, Polish, Turkish, Tartar and Asian coins. This unique collection of coins had been amassed by Stanzani in Russia, where he had spent most of his life. Of particular interest and value are the cut stones with amethysts, topaz, aquamarine, white quartz, cornelian and a group of agates enclosed in a small book-shaped case.

Silver "Campanian Roman Didrachm" (265 BC), with Hercules with club and the lion's skin tied around his neck on the obverse and the She-wolf nursing the twins on the reverse, and with the words "*ROMANO(rum)*" in exergue. From the Bignami Collection

Gold half-stater coin, from the so-called "oath" series. Head of two-faced Janus on the obverse, and oath scene on reverse. "*ROMA*" in exergue (225-217 BC). From the Bignami Collection

Bignami Collection
In 1897 the Archaeological Commission acquired the Bignami Collection, which consisted of 2,225 coins minted during the Roman Republican age. Giulio Bignami began his collection in 1879, collecting coins from vaults and collections put up for public auction or acquiring them without any mediation. Those belonging to Giovanni Guidi of Bologna, Nicola Bellini of Campobasso and Baxter belonged to the latter group. Giulio Bignami also had the hindsight to purchase some of the pieces from the Bartolomeo Borghesi Collection at a public auction in Rome in 1893. After selling the collection to the Medal Collection, Bignami continued enriching the sector with further donations of coins he purchased on the antique market.

An Agustan aureus,
with emperor's effigy
on the obverse; on reverse
star-sign of Capricorn, under
which sign Augustus maintained
his birthday fell; Colonia Patricia
Spanish mint (18-16 BC).
From the Campana Collection

Trajan aureus with emperor's
effigy on the obverse; on reverse,
image of the Trajan's Forum,
in memory of the emperor's grand
building schemes, Roman mint
(112-114 AD).
From the Campana Collection

Campana Collection

The Campana Collection is one of the most important parts of the numismatic
collections of the Municipality of Rome.

It became part of the Capitoline Medal Collection in March 1873 and it is the only
part of the Campana Collections to remain in the city of Rome, the others having
been dispersed in other important European museums. Purchased from the Monte
di Pietà for the sum of 50,000 lire, it had belonged to the Marquis Giampietro
Campana, a famous collector and director of the Monte itself since 1832. His career
ended with an inglorious prison sentence imposed by the papal government for
embezzlement, peculation and abuse of power; the sentence was then changed into
exile and the expropriation of all his property, which was later dispersed. The
collection consisted of 456 Roman and Byzantine gold coins (only 455 have been
recognized for sure); some of these have a small eagle that it might have been part
of a collection belonging to the Estensi family.

The original nucleus consisted of the collection created around the middle of the
1700s by Cardinal Alessandro Albani. Campana then enriched the collection he had
inherited from his father, even adding several imitations so that he had a complete
series of the evolution of gold coinage in Rome and Byzantine from around 80 BC
to after the year 1000.

Gems and jewels of the Archaeological Commission

A nucleus of gems, cameos and engraved vitreous paste as well as several ancient
jewels were found during excavations by the Municipal Archaeological Commission.
Other examples were also acquired or donated during the same period.

The majority are gems from the Roman Imperial age, from the Augustan age to the
fourth century AD, mostly engraved, but there are also examples with decorations
in relief; most of the depictions are of divinities and heroes from classical
mythology as well as several portraits that convey the considerable influence
of public portrait painting.

Sardonyx cameo
with bust of young prince
(fourth century AD).
From purchases and excavations
by the Archaeological Commission

Sardonyx cameo with veiled Livia
and, facing her, another person
from the Imperial family
(Augustus?).
From purchases and excavations
by the Archaeological Commission

Coins of the Archaeological Commission
Over 45,000 coins were added to the Capitoline Medal Collection as a result of
the supervision of the excavations carried out for the public works for the urban
transformation of Rome and as a result of the purchases and donations of the
Municipal Archaeological Commission, which was founded in 1872.
However, the information regarding their origins has unfortunately been lost
for most of the finds from the excavations, since the numismatic material was
described in only very generic terms in both the reports by the Commission
inspectors and in the entrance registers of the Capitoline collections.
It was therefore possible to trace the information regarding their discovery for just
a small number of pieces. For example, this is the case of the 19 *solidi* that belong
to a treasure datable to 480-491 AD, discovered on the Esquiline on what is now
Piazza Vittorio Emanuele, and also the four bronze medals that were discovered
on Monte di Giustizia in the area of Stazione Termini.

Two Gothic eagle-shaped fibulae in gold foil, rock crystal and garnets (*cloisonné* technique). Found in a burial site along Via Flaminia (late fifth-sixth century AD).
From purchases and excavations by the Archaeological Commission

Treasure of Via Alessandrina
On February 22, 1933, during the demolition of a housing block at Via Alessandrina 101 to allow the construction of Via dei Fori Imperiali, a labourer dropped an iron slab covered with two rows of bricks: a cascade of gold coins poured out of the opening. It was the treasure of the Roman antique dealer, Francesco Martinetti, who had lived in that house from 1865 until his death in 1895. The treasure of Via Alessandrina includes 2,529 ancient, mediaeval, modern and nineteenth-century gold coins, as well as 81 pieces of jewellery.
On the one hand it is made up of the money Martinetti had accumulated with the sales of ancient finds, and on the other, of antique material, which was a sort of "store" the merchant could draw on if needed. Of particular importance amongst the jewels are the gems from the Boncompagni Ludovisi Collection, one of the most important collections of precious stones in the seventeenth century in Rome. Evidence of the value of the collection is also the existence of sulphur casts of the engraved stones. As regards the numismatic finds, the presence of unique or rare pieces should be pointed out, as should the testimony of ancient treasures recognized as belonging to the collection, such as the one exhibited, with aurei of the late Roman Republic, discovered near Caserta at Caiazzo in 1877.

Gold medallion with inlaid
chrysolite depicting female profile,
perhaps Agrippina or Antonia.
From the Treasure of Via
Alessandrina, formerly the
Boncompagni Ludovisi Collection

Gold medallion with sardonyx
cameo, with integrated gold figure;
depicts the busts of two people,
facing each other, one wearing
a pallium, the other with third
century AD hairstyle.
Perhaps Imperial couple,
or private wedding portrait.
From the Treasure of Via
Alessandrina

Gold medallion with inlaid
cornelian depicting priestess
with statue of Apollo (inlay
from second half of first century).
From the Treasure of
Via Alessandrina, formerly
Boncompagni Ludovisi Collection

The Capitoline Treasure

In 1938 under circumstances that are not entirely clear, during the excavation of
the Gallery Junction beneath the piazza of the Capitoline Hill, a treasure with 77
silver coins was discovered in the area between the Palazzo dei Conservatori and
the *Tabularium*.

They depict the first Roman coinage in silver, the Roman-Campane didrachmas, as
well as coins from Naples and Taranto, several Paduan drachmas and the so-called
quadrigati, Roman coins that took their name from the type of reverse. The total
absence of denarii leads to the belief that these were coined before their
introduction. The site of the discovery is relatively close to the Temple of Veiovis
and a votive deposit that was found during the same period; a religion that might
have been linked to the sacred site of the *Asylum* existed in the area.

The simultaneous presence of coins from such different geographic areas, which
were unlikely to be in circulation together, makes the supposition plausible that
they were left there as votive offerings.

Orsini Collection

The purchase of the "Historic Collection of the Orsini Residence in Rome of Seals,
Plaques, Medals, etc. from 1300 to 1825" was decreed by the Municipal Council
in 1902.

The collection consisted of 93 pieces, including rare medals, small plaques and
seals in metal and cornelian from between the fourteenth and nineteenth century.
Some of the seals are extremely simple, belonging to figures who were protagonists
in the historic events of the city of Rome, while others are more elaborate and
valuable, the property of the last Dukes of Bracciano, Prince Flavio and his second
wife Anna Maria della Tremouille. Of great rarity are the medals dedicated to Paolo
Giordano II, one of the most interesting figures in the seventeenth century – a poet,
philosopher, musician, inventor of the water organ and satirical drawer. He
engraved medals with the portrait of himself and his wife Isabella. There is also a
numerous group of medals coined during the pontificate of Benedict XIII Orsini
(1724-1730), which, as regards completeness, makes the collection second only to
that of the Vatican Medal Collection.

Gold medal coined by the Municipality for the 2,725th anniversary of the founding of Rome (April 21, 1972) celebrating the 500th anniversary of the opening of the Capitoline Museums to the general public

Collection of "*solfi*" (sulphur casts) depicting some of the jewels in the Boncompagni Ludovisi Collection

Small treasure-trove of Caesarian aurei minted on behalf of Aulus Hirtius (46 BC). From the Treasure of Via Alessandrina

New accessions

During the years immediately following the Second World War, the Medal Collections were enriched with donations and purchases.

Amongst the most significant donations are those by Eugenio Di Castro of Roman "assi" of the Republic, perhaps from a treasure, and by Baron Jordanov of "kopeki" issued shortly before the Russian Revolution.

Noteworthy is also the purchase in 1954 of some rare coins of the Roman Senate, minted by Senator Brancaleone d'Andalò between 1253 and 1256, from a large collection belonging to Angelo Signorelli. Chronologically, the last acquisition was the donation to the Capitoline Medal Collection by the Association "Friends of the Museums of Rome" in 1994, of a box of red sulphur casts of the cameos and engraved gems from the Boncompagni Ludovisi Collection. From the second half of the eighteenth century and containing 61 "*solfi*," the box was part of a large collection of casts belonging to the Count of Beverley, which was sold in London in 1990.

Medals and decorations

The Capitoline Medal Collection also houses a collection of medals and decorations of diverse kinds and origins, many of which were either donated or purchased. It houses a collection of the "Metallic history of the Savoia Lineage" of Loevy, and a series of medals by the Girometti engravers, as well as other commemorative examples of different kinds, in particular regarding those that were more directly linked to the life of the modern and contemporary city.

Particularly worthy of mention is the series of the yearly medals of the Municipality of Rome, coined in the three metals (gold, silver and bronze) by the State Mint (institution designated to public documents). Famous sculptors or medallists were commissioned with their creation to celebrate events and figures that were of importance to the city and nation. Other periodical coinages of the Municipality of Rome are those for the *Cultori di Roma* and those coined for the Presidency of the Municipal Council.

The central portion
of the terracotta pediment from
Via di San Gregorio, reassembled
in the museum

Hall of the Pediment

The hall houses the reconstruction of the polychrome terracotta pediment of a temple
from the middle of the second century BC, the fragments of which were discovered at
the end of the nineteenth century in Via di San Gregorio, in the valley between
Palatine and Caelian, below a layer with the remains of the Neronian fire of 64 AD.
On the basis of iconographic analysis, the temple in question has been hypothetically
identified as that of the *Fortuna Respiciens* on the Palatine or with a Temple of Mars
on Caelian. It is the most complete example of a closed terracotta pediment of the
late-Republican age to have been found in Rome until now. The pediment relief
depicts a scene of sacrifice being celebrated before Mars and two deities of disputed
identity, one sitting on an altar while the other is leaning against a baluster, with an
offerer wearing a toga, towards whom six animals are being led by three bare-chested
servants from the two ends of the pediment. The lively polychromy marks all the
figures that stand out against the black painted background as if in an empty space.
The work was conceived to be viewed from below: the various elements, shaped by
hand, gain in prominence as they go up to the round of the upper part of the figures.

Acroterial relief with Heracles
and the sea monster

The roof weatherings on the façade were decorated by a multicolored cornice,
the pediment *sima*, consisting of *baccellatura*, i.e. ornamental decorations, attached
to the external edge of the final tegula; on the top was a small-sized figure relief
depicting the fight of a young Hercules with a sea monster to free Hesione,
the daughter of the king of Troy Laomedon and sister of Priam.

Caravaggio,
Saint John the Baptist,
circa 1602

The Capitoline Picture Gallery

The creation of the Capitoline Picture Gallery represents one of the most significant and famous examples of the pontifical government's patronage in the eighteenth century. The Picture Gallery is the result of Pope Benedict XIV's intelligent, cultural policy, focused on the defense of the Roman artistic patrimony. Cardinal Silvio Valenti Gonzaga, Secretary of State and a famous collector, skillfully exploited the possibility of purchasing two of the most significant Roman collections. They belonged to the marquises Sacchetti and the Pio princes. The cardinal acquired these collections by sustaining the importance of their protection (in order to prevent the dispersion of the two prestigious collections) and by sustaining that they were didactic instruments.

In fact, the School of the Nude of the Academy of San Luca was established on the Capitoline Hill with the Picture Gallery. This school allowed young artists to study directly works from the past.

The Sacchetti had to sell a conspicuous part of their noteworthy collection of paintings in order to pay their creditors. Valenti Gonzaga conducted the negotiations and on January 3, 1748 acquired 187 paintings. A short time later, Prince Giberto Pio asked the pope for permission to transfer the family collection of paintings to Spain (with the obvious intention of selling it). The pope authorized the prince, under the condition that the pope could choose some of the paintings. By doing so, he demonstrated his firm intent to impede the departure of a conspicuous number of paintings from Rome. Therefore, in 1750, the prince had to yield to the pope a fourth (i.e., 126 paintings) of his collection.

The current Halls of Saint Petronilla (Sacchetti) and of Pietro da Cortona (Pio) were built specifically to house the two collections. In 1818, some adjustments were made on the original collection dating to the middle of the eighteenth century, according to the decision to move to the Capitoline collections the large altar-piece with Guercino's *Burial of Saint Petronilla*. Its arrival necessitated the relocation of some works of art of the Capitoline collections to the Vatican Picture Gallery and the Academy of San Luca. Some important acquisitions made between the nineteenth and twentieth centuries compensated for the loss of these works. Among the new purchases is a small but precious group of paintings on wooden panels dating to the fourteenth and fifteenth centuries, originally in the Sterbini Collection.

Thanks to some donations, the patrimony of the Capitoline collection also currently consists of important, valuable groups of decorative and applied art. They are the Cini legacy of porcelain and Roman furniture of the seventeenth century, the legacy of Primoli, consisting of paintings and furniture of the eighteenth century, and finally, the Mereghi donation of porcelain from the Far East. In the last decades, other donations and remarkable purchases have contributed to enrich the nature of the Picture Gallery.

Central Italy from the Middle Ages to the Renaissance

The room contains paintings on wooden panels, dating from the late Middle Ages to the sixteenth century. They attest to the major changes that took place in Italian painting from the fourteenth century onwards. The subject of these works of art is almost always religious. In addition, different formats of the paintings demonstrate the variety in production. In the case of the mediaeval paintings, there are several examples of fragments of polyptychs (works of large dimension designated for altars). In these works, images of saints or famous episodes from religious history frame the central panels dedicated to Christ or Mary. Such is the case of the *Magdalene* and *Saint Bartholomew* by Bartolomeo Bulgarini of Siena (cited between 1337 to 1378). In comparison, the Florentine painting on a wooden panel, *Coronation of Mary*, was probably the upper part (cyma) of a far vaster composition. Sixteenth century works demonstrate how rapid the diffusion of pictorial novelties of the early Renaissance was in different Italian cities.

Niccolò di Pietro Gerini
(Florence, between 1368 and 1416)

Trinity
The work was made for the merchant from Prato, Francesco Datini, depicted with his wife in the lower part of the painting. He is recognizable by his coat of arms. The overt lack of proportion was a desired effect, as a sign of humility before divine personages.

Cola dell'Amatrice (Nicola Filotesio, Amatrice 1480 - Ascoli Piceno 1547)

Death and Assumption of Mary
It was originally in the Church of San Domenico in Ascoli Piceno. The subject, transmitted by the apocryphal writings, was very diffuse, and the Dominican order was committed to the propagation of the cult of Mary.

Francesco Francia and
Bartolomeo Passerotti

Presentation at the Temple
(previous page)
The painting, initiated by Francia (Bologna 1450-1517) (probably for a church in Bologna), has the classic shape of an altar-piece. With the death of the artist, the piece remained unfinished. Years later, Passerotti (Bologna 1529-1592) completed the painting, with some modifications, including the transformation of the client, kneeling on the right, into a depiction of Saint Jerome with the lion.

The sixteenth century in Ferrara

Ferrara was a lively cultural town (it is enough to consider Ludovico Ariosto and Torquato Tasso) and the capital of the seigniory of the Estensi. In 1598, the Church annexed the city. Due to the town's geographical position, the paintings from Ferrara are characterized by a combination of Venetian artistic preferences, based on a bright chromatic scale, and a soundly composed design, characteristic of central Italian production. Direct analysis of the works of Titian and Raphael enabled the main artists from Ferrara to paint works with great evocative charm and attention to detail. The presence of well-established workshops – Garofalo's was the main one – contributed to the dissemination of sophisticated discernment.

Garofalo (Benvenuto Tisi,
Garofalo circa 1476 - Ferrara 1559)

Annunciation
The date 1528 is legible on the right
and above the fireplace. The three
carnations in the foreground are an
overt reference to the artist's
nickname. The magnificence of the
Archangel Gabriel's garments
contrasts with the simplicity of Mary,
depicted in domestic intimacy. The
diagonal constituted by the three
figures of the Trinity (the Father,
Infant Jesus with the symbols of the
Passion, and the dove of the Holy
Spirit), cuts across the solid spatial
structure of the painting, enhanced
by the central columns.

Dosso Dossi (Giovanni Luteri, ?
circa 1489 - Ferrara 1542)

The Holy Family
The great altar-piece was painted
around 1527 for a church of
Ferrara. The altar-piece draws
attention to the loving relationship
(depicted with lively, naturalistic
emphasis) among Mary, the Infant
Jesus, and Saint Joseph.
Mary's graceful pose derives
from a solid, imposing structure,
enhanced by the balanced,
colored nuances of her garments.

Scarsellino (Ippolito Scarsella,
Ferrara circa 1550 - 1620)

Adoration of the Magi
The painter was the last
protagonist of the most important
artistic period in Ferrara. This circa
seventeenth century canvas
recalls the artistic tradition of
Ferrara, as much as that of
Venetian painting and the new
Bolognese motifs. The Holy Family
is depicted in an architectural
setting, rather than in the usual
stable.

Venice and its territory: the sixteenth century

The Turkish conquests and the discovery of America caused the abrupt interruption of Venice's well-established commercial relationship with the East. Therefore, the Venetian State (the Serenissima Repubblica) directed its interests toward Italy, with obvious consequences on its artistic production. In a short time, Venice became, together with Florence and Rome, one of the main painting centers. The particular emphasis on colors is the principal characteristic of Venetian paintings. Thanks to the extended production of the workshops of Titian, Tintoretto, Veronese and Bassano, Venice greatly influenced all of European painting until the middle of the eighteenth century.

Baptism of Christ
Early work (circa 1512). It was commissioned for Giovanni Ram, depicted on the right. He observes the evangelical episode.

Portrait of a Woman
The art of the inland part of Veneto combined artistic motifs of the lagoon city with traditional realism of Lombard painting. The woman, whose sober elegance and devotion are evident (note the small prayer book in her left hand), is depicted with a small dragon, the symbol of Saint Margaret, patroness of women in labor.

Rape of Europa
The mythological subject, particularly dear to the painter, is well known. Jupiter, in the guise of a white bull, carries the young Europa to the island of Crete. The canvas depicts the full range of the artist's extraordinary scenographic skill through his use of a vibrant color spectrum.

Between the sixteenth and seventeenth centuries: Emilia and Rome

The works in this room, mostly from Emilia, are a precious record of the variety in artistic production. Contemporary with great works commissioned for churches and public and private palaces, works of lesser dimensions were designated for smaller spaces as well as copies of famous works that were very requested by the market. Paintings of this genre had a very important role in the diffusion of new artistic motifs and enabled many generations of young artists to study the works of the great masters.

Madonna of Albinea
The original, lost in the eighteenth century, was created for the Church of San Prospero in Albinea (Reggio Emilia). Correggio is one of the most important protagonists of the early sixteenth century. In the seventeenth century, his classical style became a reference point for the great Emilian painters.

Diane the Huntress
The uncommon narrative skill of this painter, who created this small, sophisticated painting on a wooden panel around 1600, can be understood better through the frescoes in the Hall of the Horatii and Curiatii, located on the first floor of this building.

The great paintings of the seventeenth century in Rome

The name of this room derives from the title of Guercino's work. The piece is over seven meters tall. It depicts the *Burial of Saint Petronilla*. It was commissioned for an altar in Saint Peter's Basilica. In 1818, it was transferred to the back wall of this room. The room contains works of extraordinary importance, such as Caravaggio's two works, *Good Luck* (circa 1595) and *Saint John the Baptist* (circa 1602), and other significant examples of the first decades of the seventeenth century directly or indirectly linked to Roman painting production. Rome was the main center of illustrative culture and the meeting place of artists of different origins, at least until the middle of the seventeenth century. At the end of the sixteenth century in Rome, two new events took place, destined to revolutionize the field of figurative arts. In the early 1590s, Michelangelo Merisi da Caravaggio arrived in Rome from Lombardy and in 1595 Annibale Carracci arrived in Rome from Bologna. Carracci was commissioned to fresco the gallery of the Palazzo Farnese. In different ways, the two artists deeply influenced the meaning of pictorial research. Caravaggio directed attention toward reality. Annibale directed attention toward a new classicism deeply meditated on ancient examples and the work of Raphael. Domenichino was a direct pupil of Annibale, and he soon played a key role in Rome as the leader of the classical mode. The *Sibyl* of circa 1622 echoes the idealized models of the Raphaelesque matrix. Francesco Albani (Bologna 1578-1660) also comes from the school of Annibale. In Bologna, around 1610, before his transfer to Rome, he created a large canvas painting of the *Birth of Mary* and a painting on slate of *Mary with the Child and Angels*, proof of his mature classicism. The remarkable group of paintings by Guercino allows one to follow the various phases of his rich production. *Saint Matthew and the Angel* numbers among his first period masterpieces. At that time, his early style was characterized by shaded contours and by dense and fluid material. Once he returned to Emilia, Guercino turned towards a more firm and classical style, as *Cleopatra before Octavian* and the *Persian Sibyl* demonstrate.

Good Luck
It is an early work, created around 1595 as part of Cardinal Francesco Maria Del Monte's collection. The cardinal was one of the artist's first patrons. The subject of the painting reveals Caravaggio's new interest in scenes taken from the street. Equally new is the presentation of the protagonists, depicted against a clear background, without any indication of environment or depth.

Saint John the Baptist
(previous page)
Painted around 1602 for the Mattei family, the work seems revolutionary for two reasons. First, the saint is represented in a new pose (although it was inspired by Michelangelo's *Ignudi* on the Sistine Chapel). Second, the use of *chiaroscuro* (light and dark effects) makes the figure powerfully emerge from an indistinct background.

Pieter Paul Rubens
(Siegen 1577 - Antwerp 1640)

Romulus and Remus
The canvas painting was created
in the middle of the second
decade of the seventeenth century
in Antwerp, where the artist
settled upon his return to Italy. In
fact, Rubens was one of the first
foreign artists in the seventeenth
century that had a long, fruitful
Italian experience from 1600 to
1608. In the painting, the central
group derives from an ancient
sculpture of the She-wolf and the
twins next to the Tiber River.
The artist saw and drew this
sculpture group in the Vatican.

Guercino (Giovanni Francesco
Barbieri, Cento 1591 - Bologna 1666)

Burial of Saint Petronilla
The large altar-piece was painted for
Saint Peter's Basilica between 1621
and 1623. Gregory XV Ludovisi, the
Bolognese pope who called the artist
to Rome, commissioned the work.
The work is divided into two registers.
At the bottom, the powerful figures
of the gravediggers lower the saint
into the tomb. They are surrounded
by other groups of well-defined
personages in the background.
Above, the apotheosis is rendered
through the contrast between the
beautiful figure of Christ and the rich,
decorated garment of the saint.

Paintings in Bologna from the Carracci to Guido Reni

The room contains works from the Bolognese school created between the end of the sixteenth century and the first half of the seventeenth century. Some of these works are important examples of the religious images tied to the new spirit of the Counter-Reformation that was codified in the artistic field through the *Discourse about sacred and profane images* by Cardinal Gabriele Paleotti (the bishop of Bologna). In the same years, the Bolognese Academy, founded by Annibale and Agostino Carracci and their cousin Ludovico, progressively developed a type of devotional art attentive of this new, profoundly religious sensitivity. This is visible in Annibale's *Saint Francis Adores the Crucifix* (circa 1585) and Ludovico Carracci's painting of the same subject (Bologna, 1555-1609), *The Holy Family and the Saints* (circa 1590), and the small canvas painting of *Saint Cecilia* (1603-1605). Many of Guido Reni's paintings and those related to his close circle are on display in this room. The artist, who arrived in Rome in 1599, had attended the academy of the Carracci. Later, he preferred to return to Bologna to pursue his form of classicism. Guido Reni's research of the ideal beauty finally reached a picture free of any attempt to imitate the external reality, as his last works displayed in this room attest: *Blessed Soul, Girl with a Crown, Lucretia, Cleopatra, Jesus* and *Young John the Baptist*.

Guido Reni
(Bologna 1575-1642)

Saint Sebastian
The work is datable around 1615. The saint is depicted in the foreground, against a landscape animated with small figures. The body of the saint clearly imitates classical statues that the artist studied in Rome.

Blessed Soul
Painted in 1640-1642, it was located in the artist's study at the time of his death (1642), according to the inventory of goods.
Here, the religiousness of Guido found expression in a pure, abstract image that depicted the soul ascending into heaven toward the divine light. The beauty of the nude, which rests on the curve of the globe, echoes ancient models.

Girl with a Crown
It is difficult to identify the figure in this painting. Without a doubt, it is one of the most exceptional final works of this artist. The pose and the drapery of the garments are based on an ancient sculpture. The image embodies Reni's last paintings with evocative power. Agile brushstrokes and the absence of color make this figure seem almost without substance.

Baroque paintings: Pietro da Cortona and his circle

Baroque was born around the 1630s, out of the intense Roman cultural environment of the first decades of the seventeenth century. The term "Baroque" is generic and defines a complex derivation from classicism. The main season of Baroque coincides with the papacy of Urban VIII Barberini. He personally was involved in the programmatic selection of artists and remarkable urban and decorative enterprises. The exceptional career of Gian Lorenzo Bernini as a sculptor and architect corresponds to Pietro da Cortona's painting endeavors. Da Cortona was the first authentic representative of the new style. The room contains a significant number of Pietro da Cortona's works commissioned for the Sacchetti family, beginning with the first period of his extended stay in Rome. In 1612, the artist departed from his native Tuscany and arrived in Rome, where, later, he became head of an important workshop. Giovanni Maria Bottalla (Savona, 1613-1644), follower of Pietro, produced two large paintings of biblical content: *Meeting between Esau and Job* and *Joseph Sold by his Brothers*, completed around 1640. Giovanni Francesco Romanelli (Viterbo, 1610-1662), one of Pietro's greatest pupils, painted the *Rape of Helen* in circa 1631, and the very beautiful *David* in circa 1640. The latter attests to his definite autonomy from his master's style, in favor of a refined, personal classicism.

Sacrifice of Polyxena
The work is dated around 1624. It represents an important attempt in the creation of paintings of large dimensions. The dramatic subject of the Trojan heroine, Priam's daughter, was derived from successive reworkings of Homeric poems. The scene is composed of three groups of figures symmetrically distributed and lined up parallel to the background. A nocturnal light illuminates a background full of barely visible trees and architecture. The consistency of the painting material is exceptionally thick.

Rape of the Sabines
The episode, narrated by Plutarch and Titus Livy, depicts the legendary origins of Rome. The artist represented the scene in a way entirely different from the *Sacrifice of Polyxena*. Here, symmetry is abandoned in favor of dynamic and centrifugal movement, and the entire composition is based on diagonal lines. Pietro da Cortona reaches his stylistic maturity in this work. The painting, completed in circa 1630, rightly is considered the first "manifestation" of Baroque painting.

Portrait of Urban VIII
(previous page)
The Sacchetti family's social status increased through the nomination of Maffeo Barberini (named Urban VIII) for the papacy in 1623. This painting, executed around 1626-1627, attests to the fellowship between the Barberini and Sacchetti families. They commissioned Pietro to paint a portrait of their protector.

Artistic trends in Rome during the seventeenth century

This room contains works that compare with those in the Halls of Saint Petronilla, Pietro da Cortona, and the Cini Gallery. The exhibited works date between the third and sixth decades of the seventeenth century. They are ascribable to the intense period of Roman Baroque art production. As already mentioned Rome was a place of meeting, formation, and study of artists from different places during the first half of the seventeenth century. For example, the French François Perrier executed two paintings of biblical content: *Moses Draws Water from the Rock* and *Adoration of the Golden Calf*. From Ticino, Pier Francesco Mola created *Diane and Endymion*. From Emilia, Giovanni Lanfranco was commissioned to paint *Erminia among the Shepherds*, and Emilio Savonanzi created the *Death of Adonis*. Some small paintings attest to the taste developed in the first period of the seventeenth century for the ideal landscape genre. The highest expression of this genre occurs in the works of Annibale Carracci and Domenichino. Giovanni Battista Viola and Pietro Paolo Bonzi, who painted works displayed in this room, became specialists in this trend.

François Perrier
(Selins 1590 - Paris 1650)

Pier Francesco Mola
(Coldrerio 1612 - Rome 1666)

Moses Draws Water from the Rock
and *Adoration of the Golden Calf*
These are two companion
paintings of sacred history made
around 1641-1642 and
commissioned by Cardinal Giulio
Sacchetti. The artist reworked
figures created by the most
important masters of the epoch,
especially Pietro da Cortona and
Poussin, in the execution of these
two monumental paintings. In
these works, the complexity of
the composition accompanies
the refined chromatic study.

Diane and Endymion
Around 1660, Bonaventura
Argenti, musician of the Papal
Chapel, commissioned the work.
A romantic atmosphere permeates
this nocturnal scene. The moon
(Diane) looks down upon the
shepherd Endymion, who sleeps.
Jupiter gave him eternal sleep in
exchange for eternal youth.
Mola is one of the most famous
representatives of the neo-
Venetian trend, evident in this
work.

Pierre Subleyras,
*Portrait of Cardinal
Silvio Valenti Gonzaga*

Cini Gallery

This room derives its name from the legacy (in 1880) of the Roman Count
Francesco Cini. He donated his rich collection of porcelain and furniture to the
Municipality of Rome. In the different sectors of the gallery, the paintings are
clustered according to genre. Next to the *exedra* with the glass display cases
containing Chinese porcelain Flemish and Dutch works are displayed: the
Crucifixion by Gabriel Metsu (Leyden 1629 - Amsterdam 1667), the *Triumph of the
Cross* by Leonard Bramer (Delft 1596-1674), and some small landscapes. These
panoramic scenes attest to the diffusion of this particular pictorial genre in
Northern Europe. The works displayed on the left wall before the columns belong
to the paintings of this genre. *Farmers* by Michael Sweerts (Brussels 1618 - Goa
1664) and *Dance of the Farmers* by Michelangelo Cerquozzi (Rome 1602-1660)
demonstrate the new attention to scenes of daily life and simple people. The *Witch*
and *Soldier* by Salvator Rosa (Naples 1615 - Rome 1673) date to the middle of the
seventeenth century. Gaspar Van Wittel's (Amersfoort 1653 - Rome 1736) ten works
belong to the genre of "vedutismo" (city views). It spread in the eighteenth century.
Van Wittel's series of seven *Views of Rome* executed in tempera colors on
pergamene parchment is especially prestigious. The next space contains a
significant series of portraits painted between the fifteenth and seventeenth
centuries. The two small works by Giovanni Bellini (Venice around 1432-1516) and
Giovanni Buonconsiglio, nicknamed Marescalco (Vicenza around 1470-1535/1537)
constitute significant examples of Venetian portraiture in the late fifteenth century.
The three paintings by Bartolomeo Passerotti (Bologna 1529-1592) depict an
emphasized psychological introspection. He is one of the most famous portrait
artists of the sixteenth century. His *Portrait of a Man, Portrait of a Man with a Dog,*
and *Double Portrait of Musicians* are works datable between the end of the 1570s
and 1585. The two portraits of Anton Van Dyck and the problematic portrait
attributed to Diego Velázquez are prestigious examples of seventeenth century
portraiture. The last area of the Cini Gallery is dedicated to the small group of
eighteenth century works. Domenico Corvi (Viterbo 1721 - Rome 1803) painted
Romulus and Remus, a copy of Rubens' painting, (today housed in the Hall of Saint
Petronilla), the *Enthroned Goddess Roma*, the *Vestal Tuccia*, and *Camillus and the
Pedagogue of Falerii*. These preparatory works were commissioned in 1764 for the
tapestries conserved in the Hall of the Throne in the Apartment of the
Conservators. *The Holy Family* by Pompeo Batoni (Lucca 1708 - Rome 1787)
echoes Raphaelesque classicism of the sixteenth century. The itinerary of the
Picture Gallery concludes with the *Portrait of Cardinal Silvio Valenti Gonzaga*,
promoter of the foundation of the Capitoline collection. Pierre Subleyras
(Saint-Gilles 1699 - Rome 1749) painted the portrait.

Portrait of the Brothers de Wael
The two brothers, both artists,
were great friends of the painter.
The painting was executed in
Genoa, where Van Dyck arrived
in 1621. He became a famous
European painter because he was
the most requested portrait artist
of the local aristocracy.

Diego Velázquez
(Seville 1599 - Madrid 1660)

Self-portrait
The attribution of this work to the
artist is reconfirmed by recent
studies. Probably it entails a lively
self-portrait of the artist dressed
in clothing that identifies him as
a Virtuoso of the Pantheon (an
association of artists). Velázquez
may have painted this work during
his second visit to Rome
(1649-1651).

Porcelain

In 1880 Count Francesco Cini left his collection of porcelain of Saxony, China, and Japan (in addition to furniture, paintings, and watches) to the Municipality of Rome. Before his donations, the works were housed in the count's residence, the Palazzo Altemps. The main group is composed of Saxony porcelain of Meissen (eighteenth-nineteenth centuries). Different series of this group are on display: Comedic masks, animals, the famous *Pastoral Idylls*, saints, table objects, and the original *Concert of Monkeys*. Instead, examples from the factories of Capodimonte and of Real Fabbrica Ferdinandea (1763-1806), and of Doccia (1737-1757), and the precious *biscuits* by Giovanni Volpato are Italian products. Volpato, who worked in Rome (1785-1818), was specialized in the production of small-scale replicas of famous classical sculptures (e.g., Dying Gaul, Ludovisi Ares, Barberini Faun). In 1801, the artist, together with his son Giuseppe, began manufacturing earthenware in Civita Castellana. A group with Satyr and Nymph and another with Amor and Psyche are examples of this production. In 1953, thanks to the legacy of the Marquis Paolo Mereghi, the Capitoline collection received an important series of Oriental objects in porcelain, jade, coral, stoneware, and rock crystal.

Tapestries

The series was manufactured by Michel Wauters of Antwerp toward the middle of the seventeenth century, according to the cartoons of Abraham van Diepenbeek (1596-1675), a versatile Flemish artist in contact with the followers of Pieter Paul Rubens. Later, a small animal, a heraldic symbol or an emblem, was added on the lower border. It replaced a written passage that was transferred to the top border. The six tapestries narrate the life of Semiramis, legendary queen of Babylon, famous for her beauty and her bellicose spirit.

The interior of the upper
gallery of the *Tabularium*
with, in the foreground,
the fragment of trabeation
from the Temple of Concordia

Gallery Junction

Excavations were conducted at the end of the 1930s under the piazza of the Capitoline
Hill, between the base of the Marcus Aurelius statue and the Palazzo Senatorio in order
to create a subterranean gallery that joined the three Capitoline palaces. The
intervention revealed an unexpected archaeological situation. The area traditionally was
identified as the *Asylum*, where Romulus gathered refugees from nearby villages to
populate the new city. Currently, the level of the piazza is around eight meters above the
ancient street level. Originating from the Campus Martius, the ancient street extended
along the bottom of a narrow valley, located between the two slopes of the *Arx* and the
Capitolium. Brick buildings in the Imperial age flanked the road. Pilasters with consoles
for supporting balconies characterized the last building. In addition, the slope of the *Arx*
was covered by brick structures related to multi-storied buildings flanking a road located
above the road in the low valley and directed toward the summit of the *Arx*. Imposing
retaining walls were constructed out of large tufa blocks to buttress the slopes. The road
originating in the Campus Martius ought to have turned toward the *Capitolium*, flanking
the Temple of Veiovis and the *Tabularium*.

The Lapidaria Gallery

In 2005 the new arrangement of ancient Latin and Greek inscriptions belonging to the
prestigious epigraphic collection of the Capitoline Museums was inaugurated in the
Gallery Junction. The Gallery walls were already used in the 1950s to exhibit the around
1,400 Roman age marble inscriptions, some of which were from the rooms of the
Caelian Antiquarium, which was closed for static reasons just a few years after its
opening (1929), and others from new arrangements in the Capitoline Museums. This
arrangement was inaugurated in 1957 on the occasion of the visit of scholars meeting in
Rome for the third International Congress of Greek and Latin Epigraphy in Capitoline.
Serious problems of water infiltration and humidity led to the Gallery Junction being
closed to the public during the 1970s, and to the gradual removal of the inscriptions
from the walls to reduce the risk of the marble deteriorating which would have resulted
in the detachment of the inscriptions on the finds.
The completion of twenty years' restoration and the creation of a digital epigraphic
database created the basis for the elaboration and implementation of the new
arrangement for the inscriptions, which had been kept in various municipal storerooms
for some time.
In the 1950s the inscriptions were mainly attached to the stair walls leading down to the
Gallery and some of them were placed extremely high up. As a result, going down the
stairs one was impressed by the quantity and the fascination of the ancient finds, but it
was impossible to understand the texts since there were absolutely no didactic aids.
This new arrangement now combines a high scientific level with the most modern issues
of visitor appreciation.

The Lapidaria Gallery.
Vault with constellations
depicted with letters
of the alphabet

Ancient texts present certain problems of approach that are more complex compared to those of sculptures or paintings: there is no aesthetic value and it is difficult to understand the written testimony and its meaning. For these reasons, the communication of information in this new itinerary was structured on three levels, which provide increasingly detailed knowledge: captions with a transcription of the ancient text, panels, and computer access to the epigraphic databases.

Another innovative characteristic of this arrangement is the creation of a specific itinerary for the visually impaired while a musical commentary "captures" the visitors at the beginning of the exhibition itinerary in the Palazzo dei Conservatori, accompanying them with different music until they reach the magnificent sight of the Roman Forum.

The itinerary

The unique setting of the finds aims to evoke the image of an ancient Roman consular street under a star-lit sky in which the constellations have made way for the letters of the Latin and Greek alphabet, in homage to the epigraphic context. The 130 inscriptions on show mainly come from the arrangement of the Lapidaria Gallery of the 1950s. Other epigraphs from the Capitoline collection were added to complete the illustration of the subjects chosen, regarding some of the aspects of the social and private life in the Roman world. At the beginning of the itinerary information is given regarding the use of the different languages in the Roman Empire, before proceeding to the world of burial, religion, law, work and games, viability and aqueducts, Roman military life and aristocracy, concluding with one of the most famous and important epigraphic finds in the Capitoline collection, the Base of the *Vicomagistri*, the plinth of the statue dedicated to the Emperor Hadrian by those in charge of the territorial districts of five of the regions which Augustus had divided the city of Rome.

Roman capital
with sixteenth-century
Hebrew funeral inscription

The languages
In the Capitoline epigraphic collection we find evidence of the use of the different languages in the Roman Empire. The expansion of Rome's power to territories with different customs and traditions led to the assimilation of the languages being spoken in those areas. The interest of the Roman State was to pass information on to as many people as possible, and this was why they did not try to stop those languages being spoken in the lands they conquered but, on the contrary, allowed the foreign languages to be included with the official State language in the inscribed texts: Latin.
The use of Greek, the language of the Eastern regions was characteristic and it was always considered to be the Empire's second language. A well-known example of Greek-Latin bilingualism is an official document, a resolution by the Senate in 78 BC (*senatus consultum de Asclepiade*) concerning the people who lived in the provinces of Asia and Macedonia, engraved on a bronze table conserved in the Hall of the Doves in the Palazzo Nuovo. The text is in Latin followed by the corresponding translation in Greek.
Examples of such bilingualism regarding sepulchral inscriptions are those of the inscription of the sepulchre of Lucius Vettenius Musa Campester and the stelae of Licinia Selene and Aelios Melitinos. Another noteworthy example in the sepulchral sector is the presence of Greek and Semitic on a slab from the Jewish catacomb of Monteverde. This section includes sepulchral and votive inscriptions of people who lived in Rome but originally came from Palmyra, a city in the province of Syria, where the Palmyrian language was spoken as well as Latin and Greek.
The four capitals and the fragment of a column from the Imperial period and reused in the Jewish cemetery in Trastevere are singular finds, of which very few other examples exist in Rome, and it was for this reason that it was considered opportune to exhibit them here. Situated near Porta Portese and known as *Campus Iudeorum*, this was where Jewish citizens were buried from the beginning of the Middle Ages to 1645, the year in which Pope Innocent X granted them new burial grounds on Aventine, in view of the lack of space and deterioration of the cemetery. These ancient finds, reworked so they could probably be fixed into the ground, show epitaphs in Hebrew, dated between 1560 and 1576.

The sepulchre
The first group of finds shows the different forms of monuments linked to the sepulchre: from the simple plate placed on the walls of a *columbarium* (sepulchral chamber with walls that have niches for the ash vases) to stelae, symbols placed in the ground to mark the tomb, fixed with a stabilising post in a hole or on the bottom of a support, or also used in the walls of sepulchral chambers. The remains of the cremated were kept in cinerary urns and ossuary altars. An inscription (*titulus maior*) on the front of the sepulchral monument indicated the name of the deceased, while the sepulchral tables, slabs with holes to pour the libations during the funerary rites were on the interior. The aedicule-shaped cinerary urn with portraits of the deceased is of significant artistic value. These epigraphic texts are a source of interesting information regarding the

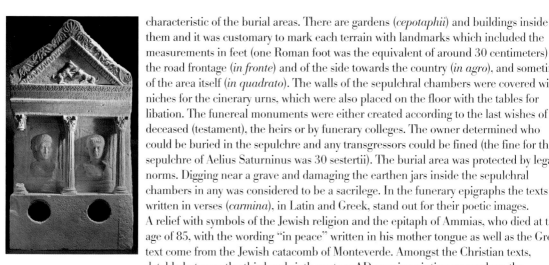

A cinerary urn in the form
of an aedicula with portraits
of the departed.
Altar with dedicatory inscription
to the Sun God and the gods
of Palmyra. The altar, offered
in the first century AD by workers
at the *Horrea Galbana*, has
a dedicatory inscription in
Palmyrian to the god Malakbel
and the gods of Palmyra

characteristic of the burial areas. There are gardens (*cepotaphii*) and buildings inside them and it was customary to mark each terrain with landmarks which included the measurements in feet (one Roman foot was the equivalent of around 30 centimeters) of the road frontage (*in fronte*) and of the side towards the country (*in agro*), and sometimes of the area itself (*in quadrato*). The walls of the sepulchral chambers were covered with niches for the cinerary urns, which were also placed on the floor with the tables for libation. The funereal monuments were either created according to the last wishes of the deceased (testament), the heirs or by funerary colleges. The owner determined who could be buried in the sepulchre and any transgressors could be fined (the fine for the sepulchre of Aelius Saturninus was 30 sestertii). The burial area was protected by legal norms. Digging near a grave and damaging the earthen jars inside the sepulchral chambers in any was considered to be a sacrilege. In the funerary epigraphs the texts written in verses (*carmina*), in Latin and Greek, stand out for their poetic images.
A relief with symbols of the Jewish religion and the epitaph of Ammias, who died at the age of 85, with the wording "in peace" written in his mother tongue as well as the Greek text come from the Jewish catacomb of Monteverde. Amongst the Christian texts, datable between the third and sixth century AD, one inscription remembers the purchase of a tomb with two spaces (*locus bisomus*), the *fossori*, those in charge of creating and selling the burial places in the catacomb, and the price paid. Other epigraphs depict symbols linked to religion or every day objects. The sacred nature of the tomb is expressed very clearly in the epitaph of Gemmula, which invokes the same fate as Judas for anyone who dares violate the sepulchre.

Dedicatory inscription
by Iovinus to the goddess Caelestis
invoking a successful trip.
The plate, from the Temple
of Caelestis on the Capitoline
and dated to the third century AD,
displays an unusual image
of two sets of feet facing opposite
directions, indicating departure
and arrival

Religion

These inscriptions are examples of devotion to the gods: from the offer to
the venerated god, also following a dream, to the *ex voto* in Latin and Greek.
The inscriptions *"itus et reditus"* (there and back), regarding a successful journey,
and the inscriptions referring to the *bidentalia*, places struck by lightening, are
particularly unusual. Since these were believed to be unlucky, they were fenced in,
hiding a stone underground, as a symbol of the lightening that struck. The sacrifice
of a sheep (*bidens*), the Latin name of which probably alludes to the characteristic
of the pronounced development of two teeth, then completed the purificatory ritual.

Law

Legal epigraphy concerns ancient texts regarding legal dispositions of a public or
private nature, inscribed on metal, marble and other materials. However, bronze
became the most commonly used material, both owing to its practical use and
preservation. To be applicable, law dispositions did not necessarily have to be made
public but at times, the *tabulae* containing them were displayed in Rome in
appropriate places, while in Italy and the Imperial provinces the publication of the
documents was done by showing the inscribed text, the copy of a sample sent from
the capital. This section includes the legal texts that go back to the Republican age
(second century BC) until the fourth century AD, referring to different kinds of
dispositions: two edicts issued by magistrates, a law and a *senatoconsulto*
(disposition by the Senate). The edict of the magistrate Lucius Sentius, in power
from 93 and 89 BC, regards the borders of the sites of the Esquiline and the ban,
forbidding the burning of corpses and leaving rubbish within the city borders.
There are another two copies, one in the Montemartini Power Plant, and the other

Sepulchral altar of an archivist-bookkeeper who worked at the imperial palace

in the Roman National Museum; the contents of the Sentius edict are similar and also regard the protection of an urban area belonging to the Esquiline is the *senatoconsulto "De pago montano."* The second edict, which regards shop owner contraband (fourth century AD), refers to the *praefectus Urbi*, the functionary in Rome endowed with legal and police power, and who, following the transfer of the Imperial residence in the East became the true person in charge of the city in the fourth century.

According to the definition in the text, the *"Lex horreorum"* (the law concerning warehouses), transmits a public notice of occupancy with the relative specifications for renting rooms belonging to the Empire.

Professions and crafts

The section begins with the *apparitores* of magistrates (junior staff assigned to them), a lictor (*lictor*) and a consular messenger (*viator consulari*); a public servant was in charge of the ritual functions of a sacerdotal college. These were followed by members of the Imperial administration; some of them held posts linked to financial management such as the person in charge of the office for the collection of the taxes on importations to Alexandria of Egypt (*procurator ad anabolicum Alexandriae*), and of the office for the collection of the tax on the legalization of documents (*ad rationem chartariam*), or an archivist working in a public office which we could compare to today's land registry office (*tabularius mensorum aedificiorum*). Some of the other duties of the Imperial Palace included a clerk who checked documents (*contrascriptor*), the curator of the Imperial heritage (*procurator patrimonii Caesaris*) and an accountant archivist (*tabularius castrensis*). There are many testimonies of private professions, tradesmen and craftsmen: from naval design and construction (*architectus et faber navalis*) to the engraving of gems (*sculptor gemmarius*) or the flower crown maker who had his shop on Via Sacra in the Roman Forum (*coronarius de Sacra via*). There was no lack of professional activities that already enjoyed great prestige (*honestae*) in Roman society such as that of the doctor (*medicus*) or the oculist (*medicus ocularius*). The last to appear is the world of the circus and amphitheater, with the inscriptions of the charioteers of the green factions (*cursor factionis prasinae*) and blue factions (*agitator factionis venetae*) and the stele of Anicetus, the gladiator armed with a sword and a skilled attacker (*provocator spatharius*).

Games

In Roman society portable boards called *tabulae lusoriae* (game boards, chess boards) were used for board games. The cheapest examples were made in wood, while the more valuable ones were in bronze or marble, such as the ones that can be seen here, with semi-precious stones and engraved wood. Many *tabulae lusoriae* were also engraved on the floors of public buildings and can still be seen today. The most common games were merrils, the game of the *fossette*, the game of the twelve lines

Base of a statue dedicated
to the fifth Cohort of the *Vigiles*
(*Cohortes Vigilum*) at Caracalla

(*duodecim scripta*), *ludus latrunculorum* (game of soldiers or mercenaries), a complex war game similar to the modern-day game of chess, and games of letter writing such as the one on show called *"dei Reges."* The game of the twelve lines was played on a table, usually made of marble; two words were written on it, usually with 6 characters each, spread over three lines with a total of 36 letters (hence the name "game of 36 boxes," by which it is also known). Three dice and thirty tiles were used, fifteen white and fifteen black; each box could have more than one tile. The player could move up to three tiles: one tile by adding the score of the three dice, two tiles by using one score for one die and the rest for the second, three tiles with the score of each individual dice. The aim of the game was to get one's own tiles off the board first, either by choosing the sum or the breakdown of the numbers made with the dice.

Viability and aqueducts

The three epigraphic texts belong to the group of inscriptions that identify the routes that can be linked to roads or aqueducts.

The oldest text is an example of an itinerary landmark indicating the presence of a private road (*iter privatum*). Whereas the milliary of Via Prenestina is an example of the same kind of landmark, but situated on a much bigger public road, one of the consular roads, informing the passer-by of the road they are going along, expressed in miles. The aqueduct landmarks, which were mainly in the vicinity of or in Rome, were made in series and were marked by progressive numbers along the route.

From the Augustan age on, the office of the *curator aquarum*, who was responsible for the protection of the aqueducts and water distribution, was responsible for their disposition while the concession of water use by private people was the emperor's prerogative.

Military

The two large bases dedicated to the fifth Cohort of the *Vigiles*, which had its headquarters in the Church of Santa Maria in Dominica sul Celio, give us information regarding the organization of this group. Commanded by a prefect, the *vigiles* had the function of a night police in the city, including surveillance against theft by thieves and burglars and extinguishing fires. The group was mainly made up of *liberti* (freed slaves) divided into seven legions, each with 1,000 men.

The body of guards was known as *excubitorium*, and there was one for each city district, while the barracks were called *statio*. The funerary stele of Lucius Moneius Secundus offers an impressive image of this military body, and it is dedicated by a soldier of the urban legion, created by Augustus as a day-time police body. Led by a prefect with the rang of Senator, they were housed in the Castrum Praetorium together with the praetorians. It was not until Aurelian (270-275 AD) that the city police had their own barracks in Campus Martius.

The stele of Lucius Nonius Martialis brings us to another military body in Rome, that of the *statores Augusti*, which was made up of two centuries assigned to the

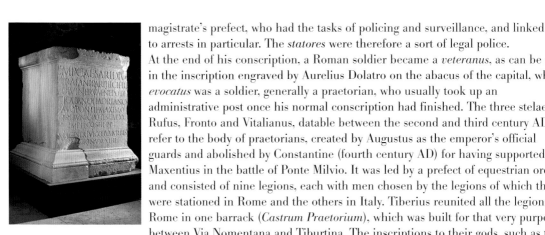

Base of the *Vicomagistri*. The statue base was dedicated in 136 AD to Hadrian by the *Vicomagistri*, the heads (*magistri vici*) of the sixteen territorial districts of Rome. The monument is particularly important historically because, along its sides, there is a list of five of the fourteen Augustan regions, complete with the name of the magistrate responsible for each. Its historical-topographic importance is further enhanced by the fact that it is one of the first archaeological finds put on display at the piazza on the Capitoline Hill; in fact, according to manuscript sources, it was at the Capitoline Hill as early as the fifteenth century

magistrate's prefect, who had the tasks of policing and surveillance, and linked to arrests in particular. The *statores* were therefore a sort of legal police. At the end of his conscription, a Roman soldier became a *veteranus*, as can be read in the inscription engraved by Aurelius Dolatro on the abacus of the capital, while *evocatus* was a soldier, generally a praetorian, who usually took up an administrative post once his normal conscription had finished. The three stelae of Rufus, Fronto and Vitalianus, datable between the second and third century AD, refer to the body of praetorians, created by Augustus as the emperor's official guards and abolished by Constantine (fourth century AD) for having supported Maxentius in the battle of Ponte Milvio. It was led by a prefect of equestrian order and consisted of nine legions, each with men chosen by the legions of which three were stationed in Rome and the others in Italy. Tiberius reunited all the legions in Rome in one barrack (*Castrum Praetorium*), which was built for that very purpose between Via Nomentana and Tiburtina. The inscriptions to their gods, such as the great plinth that remembers the contribution of twenty denarii and a quadrant of bronze from each soldier as an offering to the gods, come from the Esquiline and are proof of the existence of a place of religion linked to this military body in the third century AD. The magistrate's prefect also led another military body, the *equites singulares*, the mounted guards specially selected for the emperor, first established by Trajan or perhaps even earlier by the Flavi, to replace the *corporis custodes* Constantine had abolished for supporting Maxentius. The altar of the knight Quintus Sulpicius Celsus is unique, giving us an equestrian example of *cursus honorum* (the list of commissions) and cites one of the prefectures the knights might aspire to, that of *Genio Militare*. The cinerary urn lid of Marcus Iulius Saturninus and the sepulchral inscription of Alagria Ingenua and his children remember two legion centurions.

Roman aristocracy

In epigraphy, the inscriptions on the two state plinths are defined honorary, that is, conceived as a dedication to a person.

Both texts show that the exaltation of the work of the person the inscription is for is through the entire *cursus honorum*, the list of public posts they have held, with the additional personal qualities of the two political leaders: Quintus Aurelius Symmachus and Virius Nichomacus Flavianus, amongst the most well-known members of Roman aristocracy of the fourth century AD. In Rome the Simmaci and Nicomachi families were the most representative of that senatorial class linked to the defence of the ancient values of Roman tradition and paganism, during a period in which Christianity was beginning to assert itself the most with Emperor Constantine. The discovery of the two plinths at the "Ospedale Militare del Celio" strengthened the hypothesis that the two families lived on the hill, which has now been confirmed by archaeological excavations in the area.

Flat arch with inscription related to the inspection of 78 BC

The Tabularium, the ancient Rome archive

In the first century BC, an imposing structure in ashlar masonry and cement was constructed on the inclines of the Capitoline Hill that slope down toward the Roman Forum. The building was the site of the *Tabularium*, the ancient Roman archive. Despite the size and the importance of the construction, this building is not recorded in the literary sources. Direct analysis of the remaining structures provides the only information about the building. Interpretation is difficult because the building remained always in use. In the Roman period, maybe Flavian-Trajanic, the *Tabularium* underwent a thorough resystematization. At this time, a hydraulic conduit was installed in the lower gallery, and the staircase leading toward the Forum was abandoned. Simultaneously, a masonry vault was inserted in the Temple of Veiovis.

In the periods following the Roman era, it seems that predators and quarrymen did not destroy the building. In fact, they destroyed other buildings on the hill, whereas the *Tabularium* was inhabited and fortified. Later the Palazzo Senatorio was built on top of it. This palace was the meeting place of the Roman Senate, constituted in 1144, and residence of its symbolic leader, the Senator. The Palazzo Senatorio was enlarged and modified during the course of following centuries. Various rooms dating to the Roman period were used in different ways according to necessity. Until the seventeenth century, they housed the "*salara* of the Capitoline Hill," kitchens, stables, services for the Senator, and prisons for those awaiting judgment of the senatorial tribunal.

The rediscovery of the Roman monument began in the nineteenth century, first through the excavations of the Roman Forum (that brought to light the Temple of

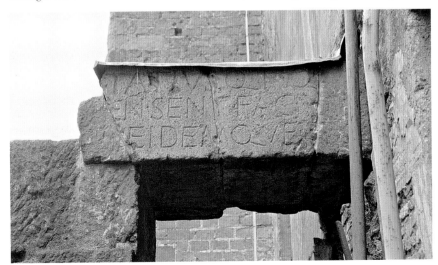

Reconstructed section
of the *Tabularium*
by Constant Moyaux,
1867

Vespasian and Titus and the Temple of Concordia at the foot of the *Tabularium*),
then through the excavations of its internal environment.
Extensive adaptations of the building were executed according to new
administrative needs during the middle of the nineteenth century. This
restructuring took place after the general transformation of the jurisdiction
and bureaucratic structure of the Municipality of Rome (in particular, after the
suppression of the senatorial tribunal and related prisons). In addition, offices were
constructed on the upper floors. Currently, they are separated entirely from the area
relevant to the Roman monument. The gallery of Sixtus IV, which could be reached
solely from the gallery facing the Forum, was part of the Roman monument.
The desire to validate the Roman monument and to connect the three Capitoline
buildings with an underground gallery led to thorough resystematization
interventions at the end of the 1930s. Such efforts saw to the opening of two
arcades of the gallery facing the Forum and the discovery of the Temple of Veiovis
in the gallery of Sixtus IV. In the last twenty years, the alarm caused by the
continual degradation of the ancient walls and the danger of the collapse of the
entire building generated many studies on the building. The results of these studies
contributed to the creation of a restoration project that was part of the larger
restoration of the entire Palazzo Senatorio complex.

The Palazzo Senatorio
in a drawing by Etienne Dupérac,
datable around 1563.
In the background, the only
arcade of the *Tabularium*
that remained open and
accessible to the Roman Forum,
as an entrance to the *"salara"*

Palazzo Senatorio
in the nineteenth century
in a watercolor
by Constant Moyaux

Section of the Palazzo
Senatorio - *Tabularium*

Internal staircase
between the Temple of Veiovis
and the Roman Forum

The *Tabularium* derives its name from bronze *tabulae*. Laws and official acts were engraved on these tablets. The building was identified at the beginning of the fifteenth century according to an inscription read by Poggio Bracciolini and later lost. The inscription, very ruined and written in ancient characters, was visible near the "*salara*" of the Capitoline Hill, inside the Palazzo Senatorio. The inscription recorded that Quintus Lutatius Catulus conducted an inspection of the *substructio* and the *Tabularium* during his consulate in 78 BC.

In the nineteenth century, Canina found a similar inscription engraved on some tufa blocks relevant to a flat arch, which he transferred to a corridor on Via di San Pietro in Carcere. This inscription only records the inspection of 78 BC and the name of the inspector, but not the name of the building.

The construction of the *Tabularium* has been associated with the fire that destroyed the Temple of Capitoline Jupiter in 83 BC. After the fire, reconstruction of the large temple was entrusted to Quintus Lutatius Catulus. He completed his task during his censorship, in 65 BC. During these years, Lucius Cornelius, recorded in a funerary inscription, probably helped him. Indeed, Lucius was the prefect and the architect in the years of the consulship and censorship of Lutatius Catulus. Judging from the remains of the preexisting buildings, it seems that the *Tabularium* substantially modified the slopes of the hill through the construction of a unique, solid retaining wall for this rise, clayey in nature. Thus, the bulk of the *Tabularium* is composed of foundation structures that create terracing along the slope of the hill. One could pass through the building to the Roman Forum by means of a steep staircase.

The *Tabularium* had a travertine door facing the Forum. The walls, in *opus caementicium*, are covered with an external veneer of blocks arranged in alternate courses of "headers" and "stretchers" in Gabine stone and red tufa.

The arrangement of the building is very complex and difficult to understand due to the loss of the upper stories, destroyed or incorporated into later constructions, and the loss of the entire northwestern façade facing the piazza. In fact, it is probable that at least another story existed above the gallery facing the Forum. Some travertine capitals in the Forum area, at the foot of the building, probably fell from the upper story of the *Tabularium*. A poorly preserved staircase that began near the Temple of Veiovis must have led to this upper story. The original indented corner of the otherwise roughly rectangular perimeter of the *Tabularium* is another anomaly of the building. This indentation corresponds to the preexisting Temple of Veiovis.

The visit
The *Tabularium*'s southwestern side, located on the Via del Campidoglio, is a solid wall of Gabine stone constructed in ashlar masonry. It is well-preserved in the area between the mediaeval towers of Boniface IX and the buttress that closes off the gallery. In the middle of the wall, two rectangular openings inserted in the wall frame a large quadrangular niche, of which only the travertine threshold was found and left visible. The openings and niche seem to lighten the imposing aspect of the

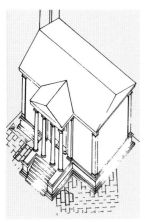

Reconstruction
of the Temple of Veiovis

solid wall through a *chiaroscuro* effect. It is possible that their presence was
conditioned by preexisting structures in the area in front of the wall.
Excavations conducted on the road in the early 1980s revealed the foundations of a
massive wall in Gabine stone, facing the *Tabularium* from the other side of a road.
The road had been found already in the nineteenth century on account of basalt
stones still *in situ*. A Republican (or pre-Republican) road predated this one.
The back wall of the niche contains visible traces of use in the post-antique period.
Recently, an entrance to the *Tabularium* and the large gallery was created out of the
niche. The gallery looks over the Roman Forum through arcades framed by half
columns of the Doric order constructed in Gabine stone and travertine capitals and
architrave. Both the arcades and the ends of the gallery were closed off in later
periods. Cloister vaults covered the gallery. The only original example of the
vaulting is preserved in the last bay, facing toward Via di San Pietro in Carcere.
Arcades divide the gallery from a series of internal spaces, three on one side, and
two on the other side of a wall constructed in Gabine stone. Wind erosion has left
a very particular mark on this wall.
At the center of the wall, a modern door gives access to a space created by the
foundation structures, located immediately behind the gallery. Originally, the areas
created by foundation substructures were closed off on all four sides. Maybe, they
were buried, at least partially. In fact, the walls are constructed in simple *opus
caementicium* without any veneer. In addition, traces of cement are visible on the
walls, left by the hundreds of wooden boards used for form work when pouring
the cement.
Excavations conducted in the 1930s brought to light the remains of a building that
preceded the *Tabularium*, maybe dating to the second half of the second century
BC. A part of this building is represented by a black and white floor mosaic in a
room that led to a possibly porticoed terrace through a travertine threshold. This
terrace had a pavement in chipped white limestone with irregular colored stones.
Excavations conducted in the early 1980s found a cistern lined with *cocciopesto*
that had been destroyed by the construction of the second century BC building.
Ascending the staircase and crossing through a narrow space leads one to a catwalk,
erected on the occasion of recent restoration. The walkway is located above the
remains of the Temple of Veiovis.
The temple, vowed in 196 BC by the consul Lucius Furius Purpurio after his
victorious battle in Cremona against the Boii Gauls, was dedicated in 192 BC.
The visible structure is a reconstruction more or less contemporaneous with the
Tabularium, with Flavian restorations. The cella is wider than it is deep and is
raised on a high podium covered in a veneer of travertine panels. The cella has
walls constructed out of blocks of *Grotta Oscura* tufa and a travertine threshold.
The small pronaos of four columns contains an altar without inscriptions. A small
staircase leads up to the pronaos. The temple is oriented to the West, towards
the slope of the *Capitolium*.

Statue of the Veiovian cult

In the Flavian period, a vault of cement construction, supported on brick pillars, was constructed. Colored marble and painted stucco decorated the pavement and the walls of the cella. Near the back and left sides of the temple, a wall of red tufa is visible. It pertains to the construction of the *Tabularium*. Because the temple was so close to the *Tabularium*, the molding of the travertine podium is incredibly well-preserved.

In the mediaeval period, a ramp was constructed over the remains of the temple. Originating in the piazza, this ramp gave access to the upper floors of the Palazzo Senatorio. The palace spared the area from the quarryman's intervention. Therefore, during the excavations of the 1930s, the large cult statue of the god was found in the cella where it originally had been placed. Turning back, one arrives again in the gallery. The space in a bay was utilized in the eighteenth century for a staircase, whose traces are visible on contemporary white plaster. The staircase united the upper floors and the lodgings of the Senator with the gallery. Thanks to a consistent fill that accumulated through the deterioration of the *Tabularium*, it was possible to exit the building towards the Forum through the near arcade, the only one that always remained open. In the nineteenth century, two large fragments of the entablatures of the Temple of Concordia and Temple of Vespasian and Titus were inserted in the walls. They represent the fruit of excavations conducted at the beginning of the century at the foot of the *Tabularium*. The fragment from the Temple of Concordia that corresponds to Tiberius' restoration of the building demonstrates the particular elegance and exquisiteness of the marble carvings, typical of the early period of augustan rule. The entablature fragment from the Temple of Vespasian and Titus depicts, through characteristic *chiaroscuro* and particular plasticity of the reliefs, a frieze with objects of cult and sacrificial instruments, including a bucranium, patera, cap, aspergillum, pitcher, and knife. A background wall corresponding to the arch originally closed off the space that houses the cornice from the Temple of Vespasian and Titus. The arch was constructed in an unknown period to join the gallery facing the Forum with Sixtus IV's gallery. This connection existed until the interventions of 1939. The cult statue of the god Veiovis, found in the excavations of 1939, was systematized in the next foundation substructure space. The statue, unfortunately headless, is over twice life size. It was carved out of a single block of white marble. The god is depicted according to a youthful iconography, nude except for the left shoulder and arm wrapped in a large mantle with wide, flat folds, extending to the ground. Similar iconography appears in bronze statuettes and some Republican coins, previously identified as the Italic goddess Veiovis. The character of the god remains unclear. For some he is malevolent, for others, benevolent. His relationship with Jupiter also remains uncertain; both have the same attributes – lightning bolt and goat – and similar names. A recent hypothesis suggests that the statue dates to the time of Sulla, and therefore, is contemporaneous with the construction of the *Tabularium*. The final room allows a close view of the backside of the podium of the Temple of

The frieze from the Temple of Vespasian and Titus reassembled in the *Tabularium* gallery

Veiovis through two openings in the wall of the *Tabularium*, made during the excavations. Turning back toward the gallery, through an opening created for connecting architectural spaces, it is possible to observe one of the spaces of the southeast side of the *Tabularium*. Two stories high, these spaces faced an access corridor closed by a wall of partially preserved ashlar masonry. The inscription of Lutatius Catulus is visible on a flat arch of this corridor. Through recent restoration, it was possible to recuperate the room's original pavement of white limestone chips. In addition, a large part of the original plaster that covered the tufa walls and cement vault is still visible. Similar features decorate the two rooms located to the north of this room, whereas the room to the south contains a staircase that descends toward the lower gallery. The lower gallery extends along the side of the Roman Forum with rectangular windows facing it. A door, later destroyed, connected the building to the Forum. The Flavian period witnessed the installation of a hydraulic conduit with a "monk's hood" type of covering in the gallery. Traces of this channel remain. Then, the gallery was utilized, possibly as a warehouse. The frames of two doors pertaining to this phase are preserved. The current pavement was made at a level lower than the original one, and the vault probably was raised. The corridor originally was smaller and particularly low. The remains of the Northwest side of the *Tabularium*, facing the piazza of the Capitoline Hill, are sparse. However, it is possible to deduce that, after the re-entrant corresponding to the Temple of Veiovis, the façade extended parallel to the south-east side.

Frieze of the internal decoration of the Temple of Apollo Sosianus. In the background, the panorama of the industrial archaeology from the Ostiense area

The Capitoline collections in the Montemartini Power Plant

One of the richest sectors of the Capitoline collections is that of the sculptures and numerous archaeological materials that were brought to the Capitoline Hill as a result of the nineteenth century excavations for the creation of new districts in Rome as capital. Another season of equal fortune for Roman archaeology and the Capitoline Museums is that of the frenetic activity of urban development in the historic city centre which, between 1930 and 1935, led to the isolation of the Capitoline Hill and the great discoveries of the Theatre of Marcellus, the area of Largo Argentina and the Via dei Fori Imperiali. The discoveries were of great interest for both the ancient topography and the quantity of materials that after more than one hundred years later, still abound in surprises from a scientific perspective. The most important discoveries come from the reconstruction of great monumental complexes and the grouping of works that come from the same excavational context to recompose the original decorative project. The result is a systematic panorama that is not only artistic, but also historic and political, rediscovering the ancient city through its modern growth and establishing an innovative relationship between the museum and the territory. One of the truly outstanding discoveries in recent years came from excavations carried out inside the arching of the Theatre of Marcellus, where there was an unlimited quantity of fragments from the excavations carried out for the construction of Via del Mare. By recomposing the statue cycle that decorated the pediment, the architectural decoration of the Temple of Apollo Sosianus was restored to its original form – the statues proved to be the precious Greek originals that were brought to Rome in the Augustan age for the building of worship at the foot of the Capitoline Hill. In view of discoveries of such importance that lead to reconstructive proposals of large dimensions, much larger spaces were indispensable for the creation of a suggestive image that is closer to ancient reality.

This was the reason for the temporary "migration" of the archaeological collections of the Capitoline Hill to a new exhibition space, during a period that was particularly delicate for the Capitoline Museums – the extensive restructuring project. An exhibition showing the monumental development of the city was established at the Montemartini Power Plant, on Via Ostiense a little beyond Cestius' Pyramid and Porta San Paolo was then opened to the public in 1997. Once the restructuring of the Capitoline Hill had been completed, the Montemartini Power Plant became a permanent exhibition area that was an extension of the Capitoline Museums and expanded the knowledge of archaeological heritage with innovative reconstructions in the fascinating spaces of an ancient industrial complex.

The history of the Capitoline Museums and the history of the first public plant constructed for the production of electricity are juxtaposed in a singular context of remembrance of the past and recuperation of an industrial tradition.

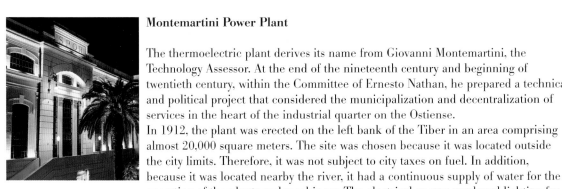

The monumental façade
of the Montemartini Power Plant
with suggestive lighting planned
and installed by Acea technicians

Montemartini Power Plant

The thermoelectric plant derives its name from Giovanni Montemartini, the
Technology Assessor. At the end of the nineteenth century and beginning of
twentieth century, within the Committee of Ernesto Nathan, he prepared a technical
and political project that considered the municipalization and decentralization of
services in the heart of the industrial quarter on the Ostiense.
In 1912, the plant was erected on the left bank of the Tiber in an area comprising
almost 20,000 square meters. The site was chosen because it was located outside
the city limits. Therefore, it was not subject to city taxes on fuel. In addition,
because it was located nearby the river, it had a continuous supply of water for the
operation of the plants and machinery. The electrical energy produced lighting for
more than fifty percent of the streets and squares of the city.
In the 1930s, with the enlargement of the plant and the substitution with the Diesel
engines produced by the Tosi firm, production increased from 4,000 to 11,000
kilowatts, in order to adapt to new public and private use. Soon after the Second
World War, a large space was created to house three furnaces that produced up to
60 tons of steam per hour. A few years later, the historic plant lost its former role
of primary importance because it was overburdened by maintenance costs that had
become too high due to its large size. New production plants began to satisfy the
multiple requests of a city in full economic growth. The Montemartini Power Plant
fell into disuse.
In the 1980s, recuperation of the industrial complex began. In 1996, work was
completed on the conversion of the plant into exhibition spaces. Acea, the
municipal firm for electrical energy and water, placed at the city's disposal the
monumental spaces in order to house the collections of the Capitoline Museums.
The conversion of the electrical plant into the second site of the Capitoline
Museums is in line with the philosophy of recuperating old industrial complexes in
order to requalify the Ostiense quarter, destined to become an important cultural
center. Together with the Slaughterhouse and the India Theater (located in the Mira
Lanza factory to amplify the Theater of Rome's productions), restoration of the
General Markets and the acquisition of the area occupied by the gasometers will
bring to completion the requalification project of the quarter. In addition, there will
be new structures for the Terza Università and the fulfillment of the project "City of
Science and Technology."
Today, commercial and production activities define the urban landscape in which
the Montemartini Power Plant is located. In one area, gasometers and industrial
complexes majestically rise, still in use and characterized by a continuous, noisy
frenzy of work. Next to this area, abandoned warehouses exist in silence. They
represent the remains of industrial archaeology that express the forgotten charm
of important enterprises from the beginning of the twentieth century.
Entering through an anonymous gate on the Via Ostiense, one "discovers" the

The layout
of the Machine Room

monumental façade of the Montemartini Power Plant, framed by two lamps designed by Duilio Cambellotti. These lamps represent historical symbols of the urban illumination. In addition, the ample Liberty space of the Machine Room filled with steam turbine and colossal Diesel engines is visible. Very delicate shapes that appear through the glass windows of the façade are barely distinguishable through the reflection of light that creates a surprising effect: the whiteness of the ancient marbles brightly contrasts against

the compact, gray mass of the industrial apparatus. The reality of ancient Rome relives in extremely large spaces and joins with another reality linked to a more recent past, still in our own memory.

The large dimensions of the power plant allowed the arrangement of monumental architectural spaces that would not have been feasible in the rooms of the Capitoline. An itinerary, composed of originally arranged exhibition spaces, equally promotes an explication of the industrial plant and the development of the ancient city. The museum offers both an explanation of the first pages of the history of Italian production, and an explanation of the urban growth of Rome through examples that appear on the ground floor (Column Room), and in the two halls on the first floor (Machine Room and Furnace Room).

Column Room

Pilasters of reinforced concrete that support the furnaces located on the floor above designate the large space. The coal slags for the furnaces were placed in hoppers, pyramid-like funnels, made in the ceiling and still visible today. Trolleys collected the byproducts of combustion. Then, the slags were carried away to be used for drainage in parks and gardens.

In this room, furnished with a continual veneer to cover the pilasters and create an itinerary, precious archaeological testimonies introduce the culture of the Republican age and express the climate of the great military conquests and lively campaigns of propaganda, as can be seen in a fresco from a tomb on the Esquiline. The dedication of religious buildings from the most famous generals of the late Republican age marks a change in the monumentalization of the city, as attested in some *peperino* sculptures that decorated a Temple of Hercules on the Via Tiburtina. Marcus Minucius dedicated this temple in 217 BC after his victory over Hannibal. At the end of the room is a small space, documenting sensitive social modifications that responded to the great conquests of the Greek East. Changes are recorded through the introduction in the private sphere of furniture, mosaics, and works of art. They became powerful symbols of an emerging class, always richer, due to spoils of war and military profit. Cinerary urns made out of prestigious Egyptian alabaster, beds made in bronze inlay and ivory and very refined mosaics demonstrate the owner' social status.

A long gallery of private portraits expresses the marked individualism and the desire of self-representation that characterized the crisis of the late-Republican society. Freedmen, proud of being Roman citizens and representatives of the small middle-class, wanted to be depicted in austere and majestic poses. The statue of the Togate Barberini and numerous portraits and reliefs on family tombs represent examples of this phenomenon.

The exhibit of this room terminates with the portraits of famous personages and of the protagonists of the politics of the first century BC: Caesar, Augustus, Agrippa, and Virgil.

The military enterprises of the deceased are narrated on four registers. Maybe they are related to an episode of the Samnite wars of the first half of the third century BC. Quintus Fabius and Marcus Fannius were the protagonists of the wars, and they are depicted in the central area of the fresco. The fresco reproduces motifs of triumphal paintings carried in the triumphal procession in Rome behind the victorious general. Together with the spoils of war that were carried to the Temple of Capitoline Jupiter, the triumphal paintings illustrated, in continuous narrative, the military exploits. Fabius Pictor, between the end of the fourth and beginning of the third century BC, was the master of this artistic genre. This artist, and possibly the owner of the tomb, belonged to the powerful aristocratic family of the Fabii.

Peperino statue
of a female figure with babies

The statue, together with the
heads of a barbarian and two male
figures with a strongly pathetic
expression, belonged to the
decoration of a religious building,
maybe the Temple of Hercules
on the Via Tiburtina. The base
of a donation dedicated by Marcus
Minucius in 217 BC after his
victory over Hannibal is related to
this temple. The female figure that
recalls the pose of a wet nurse
has been identified as a barbarian
inserted in a more complex battle
scene, that evoked a great Roman
victory, possibly Marcus Minucius'.

It imitates the sumptuous parade couches of the Hellenistic kings. The shape is elegant and very refined, and the inlay decoration has insertions of small silver and copper foil. The vegetal theme and depictions of Dionysus and his followers suggest the passage into the other world depicted through inebriation from wine and the Dionysiac pleasures. It can be dated between the end of the first century BC and the beginning of the first century AD.

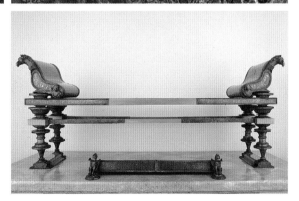

Mosaic with seascape

This mosaic decorated the tub of a bathing structure in a house dating to the end of the second - beginning of the first century BC. It was found nearby San Lorenzo in Panisperna. Various species of fish and a fight between a lobster and a cuttlefish are depicted in a delicate naturalistic manner with minute *tesserae* in glass paste. A band of acanthus spirals populated with birds, ducks, and insects framed the central scene.

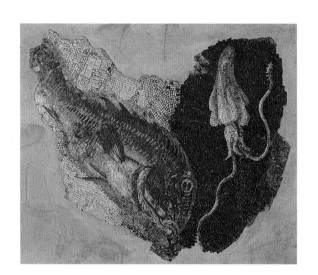

The image recalls an ancient tradition reserved for patrician families. Only they had the privilege to commission wax portraits of ancestors, preserving them at home, and carrying them in procession during public and private ceremonies.
In order to create a genealogical tree, the person who commissioned the statue wanted to be depicted in the act of proudly carrying the portrait of his grandfather (50-40 BC) and the portrait of his father in his left hand (20-15 BC).

The head of the statue is ancient but not relevant. It was added when the statue became part of the Barberini family's collection.

A suggestive plan
for the Machine Room

Machine Room

A small staircase leads from the ground floor to the most beautiful room of the power plant, a large space divided into naves by two colossal Diesel engines and characterized by a refined study of details. The polychrome borders of a mosaic pavement designate the perimeter of the machines. A socle of imitative marble decorated by festoon decorations embellishes the walls. Very elegant blue cast-iron lamps illuminate the room.

The monumental area of the Machine Room typifies the grandiosity of ancient architectural complexes. A gallery of deities, dominated by the massive statue of Athena, leads to the reconstruction of the pediment of the Temple of Apollo Sosianus. The pediment is located below the bridge crane in the most prestigious location in order to recall the Emperor Augustus' renovation works of the city and the restoration of religious buildings. During that period, 82 temples were restored and rebuilt.

Behind the pediment, the background wall of a delimited space has a large glass window that permits a view of the contours of unused industrial warehouses. The enclosed space ideally invites the visitor to "enter" the temple. Inside are the large upper frieze that depicts scenes from the triple triumph of Augustus and a reconstruction of one of the aedicules that decorated the lower order.

On the other side of the room, some of the most evocative complexes from the Capitoline Hill are reconstructed, in particular, monuments located in the vicinity of the Temple of Capitoline Jupiter and *Fides Publica*, the goddess that watched over international treaties. (There are colossal heads pertaining to cult statues, the so-called monument of Bocchus, king of Mauretania, and the monument of the Asian kings.) There are important examples of the late-Republican period, among which many refer to Sulla and his important propagandistic efforts on the Capitoline Hill (e.g., statue of Aristogeiton).

On the opposite side, beyond the monumental remains of the Temple of Apollo Sosianus, are the colossal head, arm, and feet of Fortuna that constituted the cult statue of Temple B in Largo Argentina.

The statue of Agrippina the Younger is particularly interesting. She is depicted in the guise of a priestess, and the statue probably pertained to decoration of the cella of the Temple of Divine Claudius on the Caelian Hill. It must have been part of a unitary project constructed after the death of Claudius to express the political regime and the advent to power of Claudius' wife Agrippina and Nero, Agrippina's son from a previous marriage.

Pedimental decoration of the Temple of Apollo Sosianus

The scene depicts the ninth labor of Heracles in the battle scene between Greeks and Amazons. King Eurystheus, in order to satisfy the wish of his daughter Admete, ordered the hero to acquire the symbol of supremacy in war, and that is, the girdle of the queen of the Amazons, Hippolyte. Her father Ares had given the girdle to her as a sign of superiority over the ferocious people of female warriors. Heracles, accompanied by the Athenian hero Theseus and a group of volunteers, departed from the island of Paros to the distant land of the Amazons, in Themiskyra, on the coast of the Black Sea, in order to fulfill the assigned task.

In the center, Athena assists in the combat as a protectress of the Greeks. On her left, a Nike has placed a crown of victory on the head of Theseus, who is in the act of attacking an Amazon on horseback.

To the right of Athena, Heracles moves towards Hippolyte, of which only the part from the torso to the waist has been conserved, marked by small holes to attach the bronze belt. Behind Heracles is a kneeling Greek warrior facing an Amazon on horseback who is about to attack. A fallen Greek warrior, in the left-hand corner of the tympanum, closes the composition.

The pedimental group is a Greek work from 450-425 BC, created in the climate of the Athenian culture, or, at least philo-Athenian environment, as demonstrated by the privileged role of Athena and Theseus. Perhaps the statues previously decorated the pediment of the Temple of Apollo *Daphnephóros* in Eretria. From there, they would have been transported to Rome and readapted for the Temple of Apollo Medicus near the Theater of Marcellus. Gaius Sosius restored this temple to celebrate the Emperor Augustus.

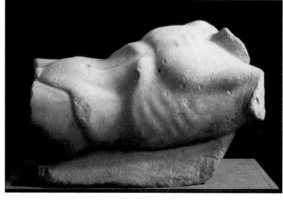

So-called Bocchus Monument, from the Capitoline Hill

This depiction with arms and trophies recalls a great military triumph. Stylistic motifs and the use of the gray stone, perhaps African, suggest that the donation was a dedication on the Capitoline Hill. Therefore, it represents the official submission of Bocchus, king of Mauretania, to the power of Rome and, in particular, Sulla. Thus, located on the Capitoline Hill, the monument honored the great Roman general who defeated Iugurtha.

The figure was created with the acrolith technique, i.e., the body parts exposed were in marble and the rest in wood covered with bronze. The head, feet, and right arm remain. The cult image was recomposed standing up, holding the cornucopia: its dimensions would correspond to the height of 8 meters and therefore also to the proportions of the round temple in Largo Argentina. Quintus Lutatius Catulus dedicated the temple in 101 BC after his victory over the Cimbrians. Stylistically, the work is a product of the popular classical style and is attributable to Skopas the Younger, a Greek artist active in Rome.

Statue of Agrippina the Younger as a priestess

The pertinence of the portrait head from Copenhagen (here reproduced in a cast) to the figure in the Capitoline Museums, allows the identification of the statue as the niece and wife of Claudius. The statue, inspired by models from the end of the fifth - beginning of the fourth century BC, was created in basanite, a particularly precious sandstone from Egypt, often used to depict members of the Imperial family. Its location on the Caelian Hill seems to secure its placement within the decoration of the Temple of Divine Claudius.

The young protégé of the Emperor Hadrian is depicted as Apollo in this beautiful statue from a large private residence discovered during excavations in Via dei Fori Imperiali (Villa Rivaldi). The sculpture can be ascribed to a master sculptor from the late Hadrian period who re-elaborated a fifth century Greek model for his idealised version of Antinous-Apollo. A delicate touch with the chiaroscuro effects exalts the contrast between the carnation and the soft locks of wavy hair.

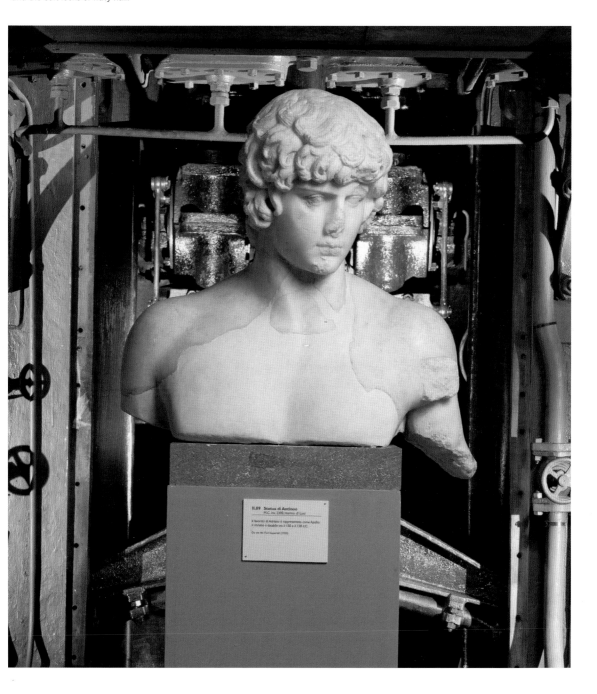

Statue of kneeling Amazons,
from the *Horti Sallustiani*
on the Quirinal.
Late-sixth century BC Greek
original that was probably
a decoration for the western
pediment of the Temple
of Apollo *Dapnephóros* in Eretria
which depicted a battle between
the Amazons and the Greeks

Furnace Room

Of the three furnaces once housed in the room, only one remains (located toward
the back). It stands over fifteen meters high and seems a futuristic backdrop made
of little bricks, pipes, small metallic catwalks and staircases. Coal used for
combustion (stored in warehouses on the upper floors) entered the immense
machine through oscillating chutes attached to the ceiling and the furnace.
As in the Machine Room, the furnace contrasts with the display of statues here,
e.g., the sensuality of several female statues, the strong modeling of the male bodies,
and the delicate carving of the fountains and decorative objects.
Through the reconstruction of the decorations of the large noble villas, the themes
illustrated in this room reflect some aspects tightly linked to the private sphere.
The *horti* are monumental expressions of public and private spheres that represent
a profound urban transformation. The development of large, private villas that
eventually encircled the monumental city center with a crown of landscaped areas
expresses the revolutionary urban reclamation, dating between the end of the
Republican age and the beginning of the Augustan age. The *Horti Sallustiani* and
the *Horti Liciniani* exalt the importance of the owner with an impressive array of
decorations barely discernable from the outside. Greek originals collected as
precious antiquarian objects, splendid Roman creations that imitated Greek models,
very refined monumental fountains, allow us to reconstruct the grandiosity of these
residences, conceived in the manner of palaces of the Hellenistic dynasts.
The residential palace is associated with landscaped pavilions, monumental
fountains, auditoriums, and little temples. Indeed, in the case of the gardens of
Caesar (later passed on to Sallustius), a garden resembles the shape of a circus
and contains propagandistic decoration that evokes the magnificence of Augustus.
The life of these new parks continuously developed throughout the Imperial age,
reaching moments of great splendor even in the late-antique period, e.g., the finds
from the *Horti Liciniani*, near the Church of Santa Bibiana). It contained statues
of magistrates represented in the act of starting the circus races and an enormous
polychromatic mosaic with scenes of a boar hunt and the capture of wild animals.

Depicted in a dreamy, pensive pose, completely wrapped in a mantle and leaning on a rocky spur, the young Muse held a papyrus role, symbol of her art. This is a splendid Roman (Antonine age) copy of the group of Muses created by Philiskos of Rhodes in the second century BC. The original polish of the work is conserved perfectly because the statue was hidden in antiquity in an underground tunnel.

Mosaic with hunting scenes from the Horti Liciniani

A large mosaic pavement was found in the area nearby the Church of Santa Bibiana. It probably decorated a portico. It depicts scenes related to the capture of wild animals for the circus games and a wild boar hunt. On a white background interrupted by schematic landscape elements, groups of hunters accompanied by leashed dogs force the prey toward traps located at the extremities of the enclosures, bordered by nets. Bears and gazelles have no escape. A man crouches on top of a crate that contains a hanging slab of prosciutto for bait. He is ready to slam the gate shut. In contrast, the boar hunt is bloody. The principal figure of the composition is on horseback. He has pierced his prey with a long spear. The mosaic dates to the beginning of the fourth century AD.

Statue of a magistrate

Dressed in a sumptuous
ceremonial garment, the figure
signals the beginning of the circus
competition by raising his right
hand to throw the handkerchief.
The splendid portrait-head
contains echoes of Theodosian
portraits from the period of the
end of the fourth - beginning
of the fifth century AD.

The marvellous Seated Girl, part of a decorative complex from the *Horti Liciniani*, is an invaluable late-Hadrian era copy of a Hellenistic model

The object of the exhibition has been to illustrate, for the first time, the recomposition of architectural complexes until now never examined together, in order to reconstruct the ancient decorative program and the cultural environment that created it. These criteria allowed the experimentation of some exhibition spaces in the Montemartini Power Plant that will be reproposed, at least in part, in the rooms of the Capitoline Hill upon the completion of the restoration efforts there.

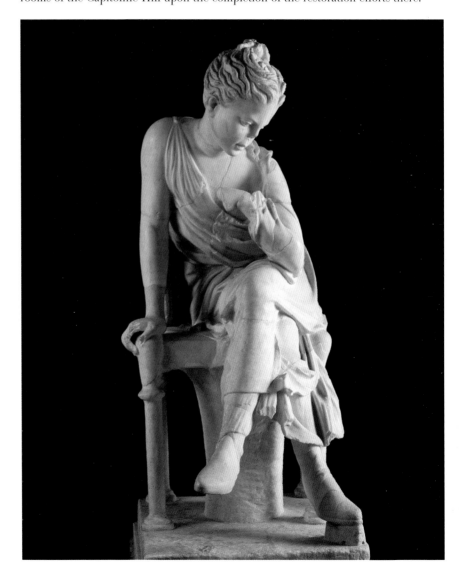

Bibliography

A. Tofanelli, *Catalogo delle sculture antiche e de' quadri esistenti nel Museo, e Gallerie di Campidoglio*, Rome 1817

P. Righetti, *Descrizione del Campidoglio*, I, Rome 1833; II, Rome 1836

A. Venturi, *La Galleria del Campidoglio*, in "Archivio Storico dell'Arte", II, 1889, pp. 441-454

A. Michaelis, *Storia della collezione capitolina di antichità fino all'inaugurazione del museo (1734)*, in "Mitteilung des Deutschen Archäologischen Instituts. Römische Abteilung", VI, 1891, pp. 3-66

E. Rodocanachi, *Le Capitol romain antique et moderne*, Paris 1904

R. Delbrück, *Hellenistische Bauten in Latium*, I, Strasbourg 1907, pp. 23-46, tavv. 3-9

H. Stuart Jones, *A Catalogue of the Ancient Sculptures preserved in the Municipal Collections of Rome. The Sculptures of the Museo Capitolino*, Oxford 1912

H. Stuart Jones, *A Catalogue of the Ancient Sculptures preserved in the Municipal Collections of Rome. The Sculptures of the Palazzo dei Conservatori*, Oxford 1926

D. Mustilli, *Il Museo Mussolini*, Rome 1939

A. M. Colini, *Aedes Veiovis*, in "Bullettino della Commissione Archeologica Comunale di Roma", LXVII, 1942, pp. 5 ff.

P. Pecchiai, *Il Campidoglio nel Cinquecento sulla scorta dei documenti*, Rome 1950

C. Pietrangeli, *Nuovi lavori nella più antica pinacoteca di Roma*, in "Capitolium", XXVI, 1951, pp. 59-71

R. Righetti, *Gemme e cammei delle collezioni comunali*, Rome 1955

M. Panvini Rosati Cotelessa, *Il Medagliere Capitolino*,

in "Capitolium", XXXV, 10, 1960, pp. 3-12

(Various authors), *Il Campidoglio*, in "Capitolium", XXXIX, 4, 1964

(Various authors), *Il colle capitolino e l'Ara Coeli*, in "Capitolium", XL, 4, 1965

G. De Angelis d'Ossat, C. Pietrangeli, *Il Campidoglio di Michelangelo*, Milan 1965

W. Helbig, *Führer durch die öffentlichen Sammlungen klassischer Altertümer in Rom*, II, Tubingen 1966

C. D'Onofrio, *Renovatio Romae*, Rome 1973

F. Prayon, *Zum ursprünglichen Aussehen und zur Deutung des Kultraumes in der Tomba delle Cinque Sedie bei Cerveteri*, in "MarbWPr", 1974, pp. 3-15

R. Bruno, *Pinacoteca Capitolina*, Bologna 1978

C. Pietrangeli (editor), *Guida del Campidoglio*, (Guide rionali di Roma, Rione X - Campitelli, parte II), Rome 1983

G. Bordenache Battaglia, *Gioielli Castellani nei Musei Capitolini*, in "Bollettino dei Musei Comunali di Roma", XXXII, 1985, pp. 65-78

J. Montagu, *Alessandro Algardi*, I-II, New Haven and London 1985

M. Cima, E. La Rocca (editors), *Le tranquille dimore degli dei*, exhibition catalogue (Rome 1986), Venice 1986

S. Panciera (editor), *La collezione epigrafica dei Musei Capitolini. Inediti, revisioni, contributi al riordino*, in "Tituli", 6, Rome 1987

Da Pisanello alla nascita dei Musei Capitolini, exhibition catalogue (Rome 1988), Milan 1988

M. E. Tittoni, *La Buona Ventura del Caravaggio: note e precisazioni in margine al restauro*, in "Quaderni di Palazzo Venezia", 1989, 6, pp. 179-184

G. Correale, *Identificazione di un Caravaggio*, Venice 1990

S. Ensoli Vittozzi, *Musei Capitolini. La Collezione Egizia*, Cinisello Balsamo 1990

M. C. Molinari, M. Perrone Mercanti, L. Pirzio Biroli Stefanelli, E. Spagnoli, *Il Tesoro di via Alessandrina*, Cinisello Balsamo 1990

C. Parisi Presicce, *Il Marco Aurelio in Campidoglio*, edited by A. Mura Sommella, Cinisello Balsamo 1990

Il Campidoglio e Sisto V, exhibition catalogue (Rome 1991), Rome 1991

Guercino e le collezioni capitoline, exhibition catalogue (Rome 1991-1992), Rome 1991

D. Velestino, *La collezione epigrafica dei Musei Capitolini*, (Itinerari Didattici d'Arte e di Cultura, 44), Rome 1991

(Various authors), *La collezione epigrafica dei Musei Capitolini. Revisioni: seconda serie*, in "Miscellanea Greca e Romana", 17, 1992, pp. 201-282

A. Naso, *Scavi sui Monti della Tolfa nel secolo XIX - Documenti e materiali*, in "Archeologia Classica", XLV, 1, 1993, pp. 55-117

L. Pirzio Biroli Stefanelli, *Una raccolta di "solfi" del Museo Boncompagni per il Medagliere Capitolino*, in "Bollettino dei Musei Comunali di Roma", III, 1993, pp. 128-136

Ch. Reusser, *Der Fidestempel auf dem Kapitol in Rom und seine Ausstattung*, Rome 1993

J. Bentini (editor), *Quadri rinomatissimi: il collezionismo dei Pio di Savoia*, Modena 1994

(Various authors), *La facciata del Palazzo Senatorio in Campidoglio. Momenti di storia urbana in Roma*, Pisa 1994

A. Mura Sommella, *Contributo allo studio del Tabularium attraverso l'analisi di alcuni documenti iconografici e d'archivio relativi al Palazzo Senatorio*, in "Palladio", n.s. VII, 14, 1994, pp. 45-54

M. Cima (editor), *Restauri nei Musei Capitolini. Le sculture della sala dei Magistrati e gli originali greci della sala dei Monumenti arcaici*, Venice 1995

E. La Rocca, *Prima del Palazzo Senatorio: i monumenti inter duos lucos*, in (Various authors), *La facciata del Palazzo Senatorio in Campidoglio. Momenti di un grande restauro a Roma*, Pisa 1995, pp. 3 ff.

La natura morta al tempo di Caravaggio, exhibition catalogue (Rome 1995-1996), Naples 1995

(Various authors), *La facciata del Palazzo Senatorio in Campidoglio. Momenti di un grande restauro a Roma*, Pisa 1995

Classicismo e natura. La lezione di Domenichino, exhibition catalogue (Rome 1996-1997), Milan 1996

(Various authors), *Il Palazzo dei Conservatori e il Palazzo Nuovo in Campidoglio. Momenti di storia urbana in Roma*, Pisa 1996

Pietro da Cortona, il meccanismo della forma, exhibition catalogue (Rome 1997-1998), Milan 1997

(Various authors), *Il Palazzo dei Conservatori e il Palazzo Nuovo in Campidoglio. Momenti di un grande restauro a Roma*, Pisa 1997

M. Cima, E. La Rocca (editors), *Horti Romani*, Acts of the International Conference (Rome, 4-6 May 1995), Rome 1998

I. Lavin, *Bernini's Bust of the Medusa: an Awful Pun*, in (Various authors), *Docere, Delectare, Movere. Affetti, devozione e retorica nel linguaggio artistico del primo Barocco a Roma*, Acts of the Conference (Rome 19-20 January 1996), Rome 1998, pp. 155-174

M. Bertoletti, M. Cima, E. Talamo (editors), *Sculture di Roma antica. Collezioni dei Musei Capitolini alla Centrale Montemartini*, Rome 1999

Caravaggio's "St. John" & Masterpieces from the Capitoline Museums in Rome, exhibition catalogue (Hartford-Toronto 1999) Hartford 1999

O. Ferrari, S. Papaldo, *Le sculture a Roma nel Seicento*, Rome 1999

Gian Lorenzo Bernini Regista del Barocco, exhibition catalogue (Rome 1999), Milan 1999

Il Seicento a Roma. Da Caravaggio a Salvator Rosa, exhibition catalogue (Milan 1999), Milan 1999

Supplementa Italica - Imagines, Roma (CIL, VI) 1 - *Musei Capitolini*, edited by G. Gregori and M. Mattei, Rome 1999

M. E. Tittoni, *Pinacoteca Capitolina praticamente nuova*, in "Capitolium Millennio", III, 1999, 11-12, pp. 67 ff.

S. Guarino, P. Masini, *La Pinacoteca Capitolina*, (Itinerari didattici d'Arte e di Cultura, 94), Rome 2000

A. Magagnini, *La cosiddetta "Tomba Castellani" di Palestrina (Roma)*, in *Principi etruschi tra Mediterraneo ed Europa*, catalogo della mostra (Bologna 2000), Venice 2000, pp. 280-289

P. Masini, *Pinacoteca Capitolina: il nuovo allestimento delle raccolte*, in "Bollettino dei Musei Comunali di Roma", n.s., XIV, 2000, pp. 125-134

C. Parisi Presicce (editor), *La Lupa Capitolina*, exhibition catalogue (Rome 2000), Milan 2000

S. Benedetti, *Il Palazzo Nuovo nella piazza del Campidoglio. Dalla sua edificazione alla trasformazione in Museo*, Rome 2001

M. C. Molinari, *Il ripostiglio di solidi di V secolo dall'Esquilino*,

in "Bullettino della Commissione Archeologica Comunale di Roma", CII, 2001, pp. 121-128

(Various authors), *Primi risultati dalle indagini archeologiche in Campidoglio nell'area del Giardino Romano e del Palazzo Caffarelli*, Study Day at the Istituto Archeologico Germanico (3 May 2001), in "Bullettino della Commissione Archeologica Comunale di Roma", CII, 2001, pp. 261-364

L. Ferrea (editor), *Gli dei di terracotta. La ricomposizione del frontone da via di San Gregorio*, exhibition catalogue (Rome 2002-2003), Milan 2002

S. Guarino, *Pinacoteca Capitolina: i dipinti ferraresi*, in J. Bentini, S. Guarino (editors), *Il Museo senza confini*, Milan 2002, pp. 277-335

D. La Monica, *Progressi verso la Dactyliotheca Ludovisiana*, in "Annali della Scuola Normale Superiore di Pisa", s. IV, vol. VII, 1, 2002, pp. 35-84

A. Mura Sommella, *"La Grande Roma dei Tarquini". Alterne vicende di una felice intuizione*, in F. Roscetti (editor), *Il classico nella Roma contemporanea. Mito, modelli, memoria*, Acts of the Conference (Rome, 18-20 October 2000), Rome 2002

H. Röttgen, *Il Cavalier Giuseppe Cesari d'Arpino*, Rome 2002

M. Perrone Mercanti, *La riapertura del Medagliere Capitolino*, in "Bollettino dei Musei Comunali di Roma", n.s., XVII, 2003, pp. 236-244

M. C. Molinari, *Un ripostiglio di aes grave proveniente dai "Colli Vaticani" (Roma)*, in "Bullettino della Commissione Archeologica Comunale di Roma", CV, 2004, pp. 245-250

(Various authors), *Castellani and Italian Archaeological Jewelry*, New York 2004

S. Guarino, *"Nel Nostro Campidoglio": Silvio Valenti

Gonzaga, papa Lambertini e la Pinacoteca Capitolina*, in R. Morselli, R. Vodret (editors), *Ritratto di una collezione*, exhibition catalogue (Mantova 2005), Milan 2005, pp. 101-106

A. Magagnini, *La collezione archeologica del MAI nei Musei Capitolini*, in (Various authors), *del MAI. Storia del Museo artistico Industriale*, Rome 2005

A. Magagnini, *Alessandro e Augusto Castellani: collezionismo, museologia e mercato antiquario*, in *I Castellani e l'oreficeria archeologica italiana*, exhibition catalogue (New York, London, Rome, 2004-2006), Rome 2005

T. Montanari, *Percorsi per cinquant'anni di studi berniniani*, in " Studiolo", 3, 2005, pp. 269-298

L. Spezzaferro, *Dalla collezione privata alla raccolta pubblica. Silvio Valenti Gonzaga e la galleria dei quadri in Campidoglio*, in R. Morselli, R. Vodret (editors), *Ritratto di una collezione*, exhibition catalogue (Mantova 2005), Milan 2005, pp. 91-98

This volume was printed
by Mondadori Electa S.p.A.,
at Elcograf S.p.A., via Mondadori 15,
Verona, in 2015